QUESTIONS AND ANSWERS ABOUT BLOCK SCHEDULING: AN IMPLEMENTATION GUIDE

Donald D. Gainey
and
John M. Brucato

EYE ON EDUCATION
6 DEPOT WAY WEST, SUITE 106
LARCHMONT, NY 10538
(914) 833–0551
(914) 833–0761 fax

Library of Congress Cataloging-in-Publication Data

Gainey, Donald D., 1944–
      Questions and answers about block scheduling: an implementation guide / by Donald D. Gainey and John M. Brucato.
        p.   cm.
    Includes bibliographical references.
    ISBN 1-883001-68-4
    1. Block scheduling (Education)   I. Brucato, John M., 1955–   II. Title.
LB3032.2.G35   1999
371.2'42—dc21
                                           98–54128
                                             CIP

10 9 8 7 6 5 4 3 2

Editorial and production services provided by
Richard H. Adin Freelance Editorial Services,
9 Orchard Drive, Gardiner, NY 12525 (914-883-5884)

Other Books on Block Scheduling

Teaching in the Block: Stategies for Engaging Active Learners
Edited by Robert Lynn Canady and Michael D. Rettig

Block Scheduling: A Catalyst for Change in High Schools
by Robert Lynn Canady and Michael D. Rettig

Middle School Block Scheduling
by Michael D. Rettig and Robert Lynn Canady

The 4 X 4 Block Schedule
by J. Allen Queen and Kimberly Gaskey Isenhour

Encouraging Student Engagement in the Block Period
by David Marshak

Action Research on Block Scheduling
by David Marshak

Teaching in the Block, the series
Robert Lynn Canady and Michael D. Rettig, General Editors

Supporting Students with Learning Needs in the Block
by Marcia Conti-D'Antonio, Robert Bertrando, and Joanne Eisenberger

Teaching Mathematics in the Block
by Susan Gilkey and Carla Hunt

Teaching Foreign Languages in the Block
by Deborah Blaz

For more information on Teaching in the Block, contact us…

Eye On Education
6 Depot Way West
Larchmont, NY 10538
(914) 833-0551 phone
(914) 833-0761 fax
www.eyeoneducation.com

FOREWORD

Readers will find this book to be much different from others, much more illustrative and practical for both the administrator and the teachers who are the front line implementers of new ideas.

We all know that change is difficult. Donald Gainey and John Brucato recognize that effecting even peripheral changes in the schoolhouse can be tumultuous. Consequently, they warn at the outset that changing something as major as the time-honored, seven-period school day is not for the weak.

Because the authors themselves are practitioners, because they have been through the process of changing a school's daily schedule in a realtime situation, their description of the steps to be taken is convincing. Their forthright discussion of "extended learning time" for the benefit of all students will be appreciated by readers who are confronting the need to give our students more meaningful time in the classroom.

School people considering major changes like to talk with their colleagues who have already made those changes. We are no different from people in other professions in this respect. We all want the opportunity to ask questions of our colleagues so that we can avoid pitfalls. No one wants to rediscover that proverbial wheel.

A real strength of this book is the authors' emphasis on key questions and the answers that follow. It always helps to hear the questions that others have asked, or should have asked, before moving ahead with major initiatives. Questions beget questions, of course, but I suspect there are few others that can be raised after Gainey and Brucato's. They are quite thorough in anticipating the relevant questions that are likely to be on the mind of every reader.

This is truly a hands-on guide to implementing block scheduling. From beginning to end, the focus is on the needs of readers, including what some writers often neglect to cover and that's professional development or inservice for teachers. After reading this book, readers can feel confident that there's little need to explore the subject further.

Thomas F. Koerner, Executive Director
National Association of Secondary School Principals

DEDICATION

Bringing this work to fruition would not have been possible without the love, support, sacrifice and encouragement of those individuals nearest and dearest to me—my wife Sharon and my daughter Robin. Many evenings and weekends were spent researching and reflecting upon what we needed to do to help improve the teaching and learning process at Milford High School. Countless hours were spent in front of a monitor writing out ideas and editing those thoughts. In the end, this book is really a tribute to the sacrifices that Sharon has made over the years in our efforts to improve our schools.

Donald D. Gainey, EdD
North Providence, RI

When the challenge of implementing Extended Learning Time scheduling became a reality at Milford High School, I was excited about the potential for us to become a better high school for our students. Without any real guide to follow, I spent countless hours researching block scheduling, collaborating with colleagues who were in the same position, and analyzing data. I hope that the joint efforts of Donald and I are beneficial to everyone at Milford High School. It is from this perspective that I would like to dedicate this book to my colleagues and friends at Milford High School whom I have enjoyed working with for many years. Finally, and most importantly, I would like to dedicate this book to my very patient and loving wife Linda, and to my children, Johnathan, Jacob, and Gianna.

John M. Brucato
Milford, MA

ACKNOWLEDGMENTS

Our gratitude goes out to many individuals. Although we have cited our references throughout and have given appropriate credit to individuals for their contributions, a number of thoughts and ideas have been gleaned from conversations with colleagues at conferences and at meetings. In retrospect, we may have inadvertently omitted some of the credit due to particular individuals. If this is the case, we extend our apologies and ask that they contact us so that we can make the appropriate adjustments.

Many schools across the nation have recently adopted some form of "block scheduling." The reasons for making the change from a traditional 6- or 7-period day schedule to a block schedule are many and varied. The questions from different sources in the community also tended to be varied and pointed. Responding to the queries in a credible manner requires more than just citing the research. Many individuals wanted to know what principals and teachers in different locations thought, and how block scheduling was affecting student achievement and many other aspects of schooling. It was gratifying to contact colleagues across the nation who were more than willing to spend time on the telephone, to fax material and responses with short notice, and to send volumes of information to aid Milford High School (MHS). To Rupert Asuncion, director of Secondary Education, Stockton, CA; E. Don Brown, L.D. Bell High School, Hurst, TX; Mike Brown, Smith-Cotton High School, Sedalia, MO; Dale Eineder, Appalacian State University, Boone, NC; Pat Graff, La Cueva High School, Albuquerque, NM; David Hottenstein, Hatboro-Horsham HS, Horsham, PA; Gary Kinsey, Clovis West HS, Fresno, CA; John Lang, Adams City High School, Commerce City, CO; Jim Myers, Farmington High School, Farmington, MI; L. Dean Webb, Arizona State University, Tempe, AZ; and Tim Westerberg, Littleton High School, Littleton, CO—thank you for your timely and insightful responses to our questions. To John Lammel, associate executive director of NASSP, and Ginny Anderson, assistant executive secretary, MSSAA, thanks for your continued technical support and assistance. To a long-time friend and colleague Doug Fleming, our special appreciation for assisting us in developing a comprehensive professional development program for the faculty and staff.

On the home front, we extend our gratitude to Helen Cravis, MHS assistant principal, and to the policymakers, administrators, teachers, parents, and community members, and especially to the students, who supported our vision for a new MHS from the start. We also appreciate the efforts of those individuals who came on board as the plan was implemented. We want to specifically mention the Milford School Committee and central office administration for procuring and providing MHS with the resources we needed to make our plan work.

Finally, we would like to recognize the people who support the efforts of the professional staff and the student body on a daily basis. A special thanks is extended to Patti and Arlene, for their technical contributions and sense of humor, and to Barbara, Bill, Charlie, Eileen, Ginger, Jack, and Mary who provided continued encouragement when the naysayers were proclaiming that "it will never work." To the believers and the converted, this was truly a team effort—Thank you! To those who continue to believe, MHS has begun to achieve a most important and fundamental goal—*E Pluribus, Una Litteratorum Res Publicae.*

ABOUT THE AUTHORS

DONALD D. GAINEY has been a high school principal for the past 25 years in three different schools. Prior to assuming the principalship, he served as a middle school teacher and administrator, and as a Head Start director. Integrally involved in school improvement efforts throughout his career, Don has served in leadership capacities in state, regional, and national educational organizations. A former "Principal of the Year," Gainey has testified before the US House of Representatives and the US Senate regarding education issues and has served on numerous commissions and advisory boards at the state, regional and national levels. He is also a frequent presenter at conferences and a frequent contributor to the professional literature focusing on his favorite topic—school improvement. He is presently the principal of Milford High School, a member of the Advisory Committee for the National Alliance of High Schools (NASSP), and a member of the field studies faculty of Nova Southeastern University, Fort Lauderdale, FL. Gainey holds a BA in Biology and an MAT in Biology from Rhode Island College, and an EdD in educational leadership from Nova Southeastern University.

JOHN M. BRUCATO, a former history and social science teacher, is assistant principal at Milford High School. He has done a great deal of action research with regard to Extended Learning Time (ELT) scheduling, and coordinated the professional development activities for teachers and staff that led to the implementation of a "4x4 ELT Model" at Milford High School. He has also developed and taught a number of graduate level courses designed to modify the curriculum and change instructional strategies for the ELT classroom. He has served as an adjunct instructor at Fitchburg State College, Fitchburg, MA, and is a frequent presenter at local and state conferences. Brucato holds a BS in psychology from Trinity College, Hartford, CT, and an MA in educational leadership from Framingham State College, Framingham, MA.

TABLE OF CONTENTS

PREFACE

What men have seen they know;
But what shall come hereafter
No man before the event can see,
Nor what end waits for him.

Sophocles

Our world is in a dynamic balance between order and stability and change and chaos. Through the millennia, the forces of change, with the exception of natural disasters, have moved very slowly so that change could only be detected when one reflected upon the past. Significant societal changes occurred at an arithmetic rate. This allowed society to prepare for changes that were somewhat predictable. However, the natural evolution of a variety of forces (i.e., biological, social, economic, political, and so forth) that have shaped our world have also produced a society that is changing at a much more unpredictable geometric rate. Ironically, one of the very institutions that is at the heart of these changes—our schools—has developed an insular organizational structure that resists change. In particular, the American high school, which has served as the gatekeeper between adolescence and adulthood, has been stuck in an industrial organizational pattern that is preparing students for a world that no longer exists.

How to prepare students for a world which does not yet exist is not an easy task. We live in an age where more youths have a greater command of the fundamental tools that governs our everyday lives than most adults. Present-day technology is advancing at such a geometric rate that the state-of-the-art hardware and software of today are no long state-of-the-art, often in a matter of days. However, changing the fundamental institutions—our schools—that have produced the minds that have given us the technology of today is not easy. If we are to produce the next generation of minds to meet the challenges of the future, we cannot rely solely on the organizational patterns and instructional strategies of the past. If we are to produce the educated individuals of tomorrow's society, we cannot merely tinker with the present system. Block scheduling provides an organizational pattern that requires professionals to rethink the teaching and learning process, to rethink what is important in the curriculum and what students will need to know and be able to do, and a shift from a teacher-centered school to a student-centered school.

The process of transforming the American high school, one of the last icons of the industrial age, into an institution that produces the life-long learners we strive to produce is not an easy process. It takes vision; it requires research on teaching and learning; and it requires a passion and perseverance on the part of a team of individuals to make the dream come true. If this sounds a little too esoteric, consider the amount of information that was available to the general public 10 years ago and the amount of information that is instantaneously available today. Then consider who has the greater ability to access the information—today's youth or adults. After considering the harsh reality of the answer, it is evident that the process of learning, the process of finding information when one needs it, the process of interpreting the importance and validity of the information gathered, and the process of using the information available to solve a problem or to answer a question are more important than the one right answer in the great trivia contest. This book is a guide for individuals questing for the schools of the future. Hopefully, the questions that are posed and the answers that are suggested will serve to release the potential that resides in the personnel of every school to make the quantum leap from the present to the future.

Donald D. Gainey
Principal

1

FROM BLOCK SCHEDULING TO EXTENDED LEARNING TIME—MAKING IT HAPPEN

There is nothing more difficult to carry out, nor more doubtful of success, nor more dangerous to handle, than to initiate a new order of things. For the reformer has enemies in all those who profit by the old order, and only lukewarm defenders in all those who would profit by the new order...Thus, it arises that on every opportunity for attacking the reformer, his opponents do so with the zeal of partisans; the others only defend him halfheartedly, so that between them he runs a great danger.

Niccolo Machiavelli

If you are considering moving from a traditional six-, seven-, or eight-period day to some form of "block scheduling," consider carefully the words of Niccolo Machiavelli. Those words were not idly selected; they were selected after experiencing the agony and the ecstasy of implementing a block schedule at two different high schools, and after discussing the trials and tribulations of colleagues who were attempting to implement block scheduling. Any type of change in the American high school is difficult. However, the amount of resistance to any change is directly proportional to the degree of the change that is proposed. At the high school level, tinkering around the edges, such as adding a new program or a new course, might be greeted with a great deal of fanfare, but such change generally only has a direct impact on a small segment of the student population. Even those changes that do impact the entire student body and the entire teaching staff tend to be of such a nature that they only indirectly impact student learning and usually appeal to virtually all of the key stakeholder groups in the school community. After all, only a small segment of the school community will argue with a new discipline policy or a new substance abuse policy, which are designed to get wayward students back into the mainstream of student activities at the high school. But change something as fundamental as the high school schedule, and prepare yourself for the shock waves.

The transition from a traditional high school schedule to some form of block scheduling can occur successfully if you know precisely what you are attempting to accomplish in your school and why. Answering these two questions helps avoid the common practice of moving directly to a canned solution, in this case the trendy block scheduling, without identifying a problem or an opportunity. As you proceed with the change process, it is easy to be sidetracked and to forget exactly what you are doing and why you are doing it. Therefore, as we guide you through the change process that occurred at Milford High School (MHS), note that we followed an orderly process, amid the day-to-day chaos and distractions within the school, which focused on our primary goals. Furthermore, note that the success of the change process at MHS was the result of the collective efforts of policymakers, administrators, teachers, students, and parents who at different times helped to move the initiatives forward. Therefore, although a team comprised of school administrators and department heads was primarily responsible for developing and implementing the various stages of the action plan, the team's efforts would not have achieved the desired results without the assistance of key stakeholder groups.

If a school is considering a change to some form of block scheduling or has just begun the process of making the change, then the process that MHS followed, the questions that we posed and answered, the obstacles that we overcame, and the results that we obtained can serve as guides to the change process. Because each school is uniquely different, the focus, the questions, the obstacles, and the goals may be different. Nonetheless, we expect that our actual experiences at MHS will prove beneficial to a school moving toward some form of block scheduling.

During the 1995-96 school year, a new principal and assistant principal joined with an assistant principal, who had worked in the district for a number of years, to form a new administrative team at MHS. The immediate tasks facing the new administration were to finalize preparations for a site-visit by the New England Association of Schools and Colleges (NEASC), the regional accrediting agency, in the fall of 1995, and to ensure that MHS was in compliance with the Massachusetts Education Reform Act of 1993 (ERA) by the act's September 1997 deadline. The completion of a self-study in preparation for the NEASC visit provided the new administration with a good deal of data and information, as well as the perceptions of the faculty and the previous administration of how well the various aspects of the high school were functioning.

The report that was generated by the NEASC visiting committee validated many aspects of the self-study and provided additional external perceptions related to different aspects of the school and the manner in which it was meeting its adopted statement of purpose and expectations for student learning (see Appendix). The various commendations and recommendations contained in the report, particularly those related to the school schedule, provided a great deal of motivation for action. In addition, the newly adopted state mandates, which were designed to be sweeping in their impact on the curriculum of the school, provided a platform for action. Not only did the new regulations define the core curriculum (i.e., English language arts, history and social science, mathematics, science and technology, world languages, fine arts and health), but they also defined the amount of directed instructional time that all students in a high school had to engage in each year. While many high schools looked to some form of block scheduling to meet the new requirement of 990 hours per year of directed instructional time, the existing schedule at MHS did provide the required hours of directed instructional time, exclusive of study halls, passing time, and lunch. Nonetheless, the MHS administration continued reviewing all aspects of the high school, the accreditation report, and the various state mandates with one primary goal in mind—to improve student learning.

Purpose, Future, and Vision of the School

Key Questions
♦ What is the fundamental purpose of the school?
♦ What values, beliefs, and norms exist at the school?
♦ What changes in the culture of the school and the society it serves will have the greatest impact on the school's future?
♦ If the present course is maintained, what will the school look like in the future?
♦ What must the school do today and tomorrow to implement the vision for the future?

We began our deliberations by reflecting on the adopted statement of purpose and expectations for MHS. The discussions that ensued with key stakeholder groups (i.e., teachers, students, parents, community members, community groups, administrators and policymakers) all tended to confirm that the fundamental purpose of schools—to educate students—has not really changed since the inception of schools. Although the words were different, the various stakeholders agreed that even in an information society where knowledge is constantly changing, we could reflect upon the notions of Jean Piaget to define our fundamental purpose. Educated people are individuals who are capable of doing new things, not simply repeating what other generations have done, individuals who are creative, who are inventive, and who can discover, individuals who are productive members of a democratic society. Such individuals need to use their minds to be critical and to verify, rather than just accept everything they are offered, and to recognize that learning is a lifelong process.

If our society was a static organization, then maintaining the status quo might be an acceptable policy. In an ever-changing world, however, schools need to produce individuals who are capable of meeting the changing demands of society. Hence, it was and is the function of MHS to educate all of the students who enroll in the high school. Nonetheless, like so many other American high schools, MHS was stuck in a time warp (i.e., living in a service economy where instantaneous global communication and access to information was the norm, while the day- to-day operation of MHS was based upon Frederick Winslow Taylor's industrial age model of the early twentieth century and the agrarian calendar of the nineteenth century). Furthermore, while it was operating the way it had "successfully" operated for more than a decade, there was little empirical evidence, other than standardized test scores, grades, and so forth, to indicate that the fundamental purpose and expectations of the school were being met. In fact, most of the key stakeholders felt that MHS was a good school. But, the lives of the students that MHS serves will be lived in the future. While no one can be sure of what the future will bring, this should not preclude reflecting upon the past, considering the present, and projecting into the future. In an abstract form, schools—past, present, and future— need to develop organizations that reflect and are compatible with their cultural environments.

How well was MHS preparing students to meet the future? If MHS continued on its existing course, it would look the same 10 years from now as it did a decade ago. How then would MHS be capable of fulfilling its fundamental purpose in the society of the future? To answer this question we had to look at the deep patterns of beliefs, values, and traditions that had formed over the course of the history of MHS—the culture of the school. At the same time, we needed to look at changes in the global culture if we are to prepare our students for the future (i.e., changes in the economic base for the twenty-first century, in the educational needs of a workforce where career changes will be the norm, in the mobility of the population, in the diversity of the population and the family unit, and in the growing reality that the United States is becoming a minority majority nation). Just how do these realities emerge in the pragmatic daily routines of MHS?

A closer look at the day-to-day operation of MHS indicated that there were, indeed, some very positive factors impacting on the teaching and learning process. On the other hand, there were some very glaring, though unseen, factors that were inhibiting the learning process. From a positive perspective, the physical facility was a well-equipped (with the glaring exception of up-to-date computer technology) and well-maintained, sprawling, 330,000-square-foot building. Most visitors commented on those factors. Ironically, the seasoned faculty and staff of nearly 100 teachers and specialists tended to focus more on the deficiencies of the building. There was a strong belief among most of the faculty that the high school and the faculty had not been given their just due in terms of the respect and the resources that were needed to carry out the quality programs that students deserved. As a result, there was a feeling that the high school played second, or even third, fiddle to the needs of the early childhood programs, the elementary schools, and the middle schools in the district. This sentiment, however, was not shared by the 1,000 plus students whose attitude toward the school was generally very positive. Within this setting, there was a genuinely positive relationship between the students and the faculty. The students generally liked and respected the faculty, and the teachers felt the same about the student body.

In addition to the formally adopted statement of purpose and expectations for student performance, there was a set of informal norms, beliefs, and values that pervaded and guided student learning at MHS. Pragmatically, these beliefs regarding the expectations for student learning were held by most of the faculty members. Ability grouping of students was a very strong component of the culture at MHS. Teachers, parents, students, and policymakers frequently spoke in terms of "130s," "120s," and "110s" when referring to courses and students within MHS. The designations were in reference to specific levels of classes (i.e., all AP courses were designated as 130-level classes, all honors-level courses were designated as 120-level classes, and all college preparatory courses were designated as 110-level classes). These designations were used as a weighting factor for each course when calculating a student's grade point average (GPA). Prior to the 1996-97 school year, there was a general track. Classes in the general track, which was eliminated based due to state mandates, were referred to as 100-level classes.

These designations did not stop with just the courses in the curriculum. Students also received an identifiable designation. Those who enrolled in predominantly 120-level classes were referred to as "120 students" or "120s," those who enrolled in predominantly 110-level classes were referred to as "110 students" or "110s,"and those who enrolled in classes in the general track were referred to as "100 students" or "one-zero-zeros." While this might sound somewhat crude, it was the norm and the routine manner of contacting selected groups of students during that school year. Furthermore, this practice was understood and accepted by teachers, students, and even parents.

Programmatically, the expectations for student achievement, the instructional strategies that students might encounter, the types of assignments and so forth, were geared toward the level of the class. All 130- and 120-level science courses had double laboratory periods, but most 110- or 100-level classes did not have laboratory periods because the lab equipment might be damaged. Field trips to the theatre or a museum were generally scheduled for the upper level classes because those students would be able to gain more from such an experience. The students in the low-level classes (i.e., the "100s"), were believed to be generally lacking in the basics and required more skill development which was frequently delivered in the form of drill and practice. Essentially, all of the stereotypical classroom vignettes relating to ability grouping were evident at MHS.

Because ability grouping and the same basic master schedule at MHS had been in place for decades, most parents seemed to accept and to understand the system fairly well. Furthermore, for a segment of the population, the system seemed to work fairly well. Parents of students who learned at a faster rate generally did not want their children in classes with students who would retard their children's rate of achievement or with students who did not want to learn. Many of these students selected courses based upon the level of the course rather than what might be learned because the higher level course would help to improve or maintain their GPA. Teachers also understood the nature of the system. Most teachers wanted to teach the 120s rather than the 110s, and the old 100s were basically reserved for the person lowest on the seniority list or the individual who worked best with "those types of students." The system was designed to cater to and deliver the best services to the best students, although all the key stakeholders agreed that the rest of the student body "got a good education too."

Beyond the quantitative aspects of the curriculum there were also the qualitative aspects of what was occurring in the teaching and learning environment. To achieve the fundamental purpose and expectations of MHS, we needed to change students from passive receptors of information to active participants who develop new skills and construct their own knowledge. All the key stakeholders agreed that students should become active thinkers, creative thinkers, and decision-makers. We needed to help teachers become facilitators in such a teaching and learning classroom. In essence, we needed to liberate teachers from the mundane chalk and talk, drill and kill, and squirt teaching strategies that the 45–50-minute period dictated, and allow them to become the creative professionals they had hoped to become when they entered the teaching profession. We felt that the academic schedule should facilitate the implementation of the statement of purpose, the outcome-based student expectations and the outcome-based school expectations in a fair and equitable manner for all students and teachers. We were also convinced that fundamental changes in the existing seven- period day was required if we were to have any substantive change in student learning at MHS.

Perhaps it was the positive interactions between students and teachers that prevented the key stakeholders from noticing some of the deficiencies. From a purely mechanical perspective, the 7-period day schedule did not rotate nor were the 7 periods of equal length (the periods ranged from 46 minutes to 57 minutes in length). Some sections of courses had double-period laboratories, while other sections of the same course did not. In some cases, where scheduling conflicts occurred, students were allowed to miss half of one class so that they could participate in laboratory experiences in another class. Figure 1.1 illustrates what a typical student schedule looked like during the 1995-96 school year at MHS. In addition to the traditional schedule, most of the classrooms looked pretty much alike (there were generally two types of classrooms, those that had five rows with six seats in each row, and those with six rows having five seats in each row). Not only did the classrooms look alike, they sounded alike. For the most part, students were the passive receptors of the instruction delivered in the form of lecture by teachers who occasionally allowed students speak in the form of recitation. The teacher was clearly the focus of the classroom. Students faced the teacher, they directed verbal responses or questions to the teacher, and didactic teaching was the norm. This is not to say that teachers were not doing their job, they were teaching the way they were taught and the way they had been taught to teach.

FIGURE 1.1 TRADITIONAL 7-PERIOD DAY AT MHS

		1995-96 Academic School Day Schedule					
		Day 1	Day 2	Day 3	Day 4	Day 5	Day 6
Period 1 7:40–8:27		English	English	English	English	English	English
Period 2 8:30–9:16		Science	Science	Science	Science Lab	Science	*Study*
Period 3 9:19–10:05		P.E.	*Study*	P.E.		P.E.	*Study*
Period 4 10:08–10:54	Lunch	History	History	History	History	History	History
Period 5 10:57–12:24	10:54–11:24 11:24–11:54 11:54–12:24	*Study*	*Study*	*Study*	*Study*	*Study*	*Study*
Period 6 12:27–1:13		Math	Math	Math	Math	Math	Math
Period 7 1:16–2:02		W. Lang.	W. Lang.	W. Lang.	W. Lang.	W. Lang.	W. Lang.

Given the existing seven-period schedule, we had to consider whether it was time for a change. Because we were interested in our product—the educated individual—we had to look to the future to determine the needs of society. In an information society, knowledge fuels the economy and shapes society. Therefore, all students at MHS need to be taught how to define what information they need, know how to find it, and how to use it. They will need to be able to envision the interconnectedness of everything. As previously noted, we wanted to guarantee that *all* students would have access to the same educational opportunities and the same knowledge and, through them, to develop the new knowledge that will serve as the currency of the twenty-first century, regardless of their origin, wealth, or previous schooling.

ESTABLISHING THE ACTION-PLANNING TEAM

KEY QUESTIONS

- ◆ How many people should be on the action planning team?
- ◆ What stakeholder groups should be represented on the team?
- ◆ How much authority will be vested, individually and collectively, in the team?
- ◆ What resources will be made available to the team?
- ◆ What personal characteristics will the team members bring to the team?

We recognized that a change in the school schedule required input from all the key stakeholders. It also needed to be a team effort that addressed concerns and incorporated ideas that originated from both the top-down and bottom-up perspective. Considering who would serve on such a team is a key component in determining the logistics of any planned change and ultimately in the success of any change initiative.

After some consideration, it was decided that the best composition of an action-planning team available would be based upon the existing hierarchical departmental structure. Additionally, there was a loyalty factor that had to be included in the equation. With the exception of one department, the members of the other departments were aligned with their respective department heads. Therefore, although the task orientation, organizational skills, problem-solving skills, communication skills, and interpersonal skills of these individuals varied, they were, for better or worse, known quantities. Based on these considerations, it was felt that to attempt to establish a planning team that did not include department heads and directors would have only confounded the change process.

At weekly meetings, the school administration, the department heads and the directors discussed the implications of the report of the NEASC visiting committee and the implications of the new state mandates for MHS. Shortly after these meetings were initiated, it became evident that an additional communications problem existed. The directors, with their K-12 responsibilities, reported to the assistant superintendent of schools. As such, some of the directors attended the weekly meetings and others did not. However, it was made very clear early in the process that directors did not report to the school administration and were not bound by decisions made at such meetings. Because it was necessary to have all members of the team marching to the same sheet of music, a change in the membership of the action planning team was in order. Thereafter, most of the weekly meetings were held with the school administration and the MHS department heads. Because the department heads at MHS represented most of the core disciplines (English language arts, history and social science, mathematics, science and technology, as well as the practical arts), they also represented the overwhelming majority of the faculty. This did not preclude directors from participating in the decision-making process regarding their respective disciplines; it did mean that they were not part of the primary action-planning team. However, the composition of the team, although important, was not the key to the planning team's success.

Ultimately, given the beliefs of the faculty regarding the status of the high school within the system, it would be the amount and types of resources that were available to the planning team that would determine the effectiveness of any plan that was developed. If we expected to make significant changes in the delivery of instruction to MHS students, then we needed resources for the development and implementation of a professional development plan for the faculty and staff. We viewed this initiative as an initial investment in the social capital and, ultimately, in the future of MHS.

IDENTIFYING THE PROBLEM OR OPPORTUNITY

KEY QUESTIONS
♦ Exactly what is the problem or opportunity that the school faces?
♦ Why is this a problem or opportunity at the school?
♦ Is it really a serious problem or good opportunity?
♦ Is the intervention within the sphere of influence of the team members?
♦ Can the team efforts make a practical difference in student learning?

The translation of the esoteric goal of preparing all students for the changing needs of the twenty-first century into the day- to-day operations at MHS along with the direct and indirect implications for all stakeholders was not as clear. What we discovered was a very traditional high school that moved along the industrial treadmill in a very predictable manner from year to year. With the exception of some minor modifications, the master schedule had not changed in more than two decades. The day-to-day mechanics of MHS operated as if everything was fine. Teachers and students reported each day; classes were held, bells sounded for successive periods, students changed classes, and report card cards were issued; rarely were new programs planned or implemented. There was a general consensus that this was just about the best of all possible worlds, at least as far as high schools went. This was confirmed each spring when a ceremony was held that traditionally marked the transition from adolescence to adulthood. Graduations were held on warm sunny days in June. Students resplendent in caps and gowns with hopeful faces smiled into cameras to mark the occasion and all was well. The formal ceremony was followed by lavishly catered parties with live bands, family, and friends. On graduation day, Milford was the celebration capitol of Massachusetts. Left unanswered, however, was the question of whether or not we are meeting the needs of the future?

A closer look at the seven-period-day schedule at MHS also indicated that most students actually had only five or six direct instructional classes per day with the remaining time scheduled as study hall time (see Figure 1.1, p. 8). Because one of our goals was to increase the requirements for all students in each of the core curricular areas without adversely impacting the rich elective programs, we recognized that sweeping changes were called for. Essentially, we had to develop and implement a plan to move the 1,300 to 1,400 students who were sitting daily in study halls into a classroom setting where they would be engaged in directed instruction. Addressing this situation would have a profound impact on the curricular offerings, the pattern of staffing, and the allocation of resources at MHS.

Operating within the collective bargaining agreement, the average teacher taught five classes per day, had one supervisory duty (study hall, cafeteria duty, or hall duty), and had one preparation period, exclusive of a duty-free lunch period. The policymakers, the administration, and the teachers took pride in the fact that MHS maintained an average class size of 20 students per class. If MHS were to eliminate all study halls during the 1996-97 school year, the implications in terms of personnel would have been dramatic, as Figure 1.2, indicates for the 1,050 students.

Adding 14 teachers to the staff to eliminate all study halls would add approximately $500,000 to the school department budget for teaching staff at MHS; this was not a pleasant thought. Furthermore, this budgetary figure

FIGURE 1.2. STUDENT ENROLLMENT, CLASS SIZE, AND STAFFING—ACTUAL AND PROJECTED

	1995-96 *Actual Enrollments*				*1996-97* *Projected Enrollments*			
	# Sec	*# Stu (FTE)*	*Ave Cl/ Size*	*# Teach*	*# Sec*	*# Stu (FTE)*	*Ave Cl/ Size*	*# Teach*
Totals	315	6017	19.1	**63.0**	385	7350	19.1	**77.0**

did not address the additional costs of textbooks, supplies, and materials. Given this reality, other options needed to be explored.

It was becoming clear that the existing schedule was not permitting the most effective utilization of people, space, time, and resources with regard to learning time. Similarly, discussions with teachers indicated the length of the academic periods in large part dictated the manner in which concepts were developed and the variety of instructional strategies which teachers could use in a classroom. Rather than helping to solve problems related to the delivery of instruction, the existing schedule was a major source of the problem. It was a means of institutionalizing practices within the school, albeit not necessarily the most desired practices, and merely as a means of moving teachers and students to various spaces during selected periods of time.

From an organizational perspective, the high school was structured along fiercely territorial departmental lines. Each of the core curricular areas had a department head or a K-12 director to whom the faculty was directly responsible. In addition, each of the disciplines had its own departmental office with a coffee machine, a copy machine, supplies and materials, and tables and chairs. While most visitors thought that this was an ideal setup, it dramatically inhibited communication among faculty members across departmental lines and, in some cases, within the same discipline. Given the size of the building and the nonchanging and nonrotating nature of the master schedule, many faculty members had been teaching the same courses during the same period of time in the same room with the same preparation period for a decade or more. During their preparation period, most teachers either remained isolated in "their" room where they corrected papers and prepared for their classes, or they went to the departmental office where they either did the same thing or engaged in fellowship with colleagues in the same department. The fabled teachers' room that is the hotbed of overt and covert communication in most high schools was nonex-istent at MHS; there was a teachers' room, but no one ever went there.

While the traditional seven-period master schedule was the source of great stability at MHS, it also was a major liability. Yet, the faculty, the stu-dent body, the parents, and the other key stakeholders had become so accus-tomed to this traditional structure that tinkering with this icon of the indus-trial age would not be an easy task. The unity of purpose among the faculty members, where present, existed within individual departments, but rarely extended across disciplines. Therefore, if a change in the traditional sched-ule was to occur, it would have to have the endorsement of the key stake-holders. The need to make such a change was present in both the report of the NEASC visiting committee and embedded in some of the new state mandates. How to make the change was not included in the report or mandated.

Although most faculty members were eager to provide the students at MHS with the best possible education that they could, there was also a feel-ing, based upon their own education and training, that the existing curricu-lum and the seven-period schedule served as the best means to that end. It was necessary to open a dialogue among the various segments of the faculty regarding the need to make changes in a system that had apparently worked well for decades. Care had to be taken to develop a change process that was both a top-down and a bottom-up process. If the new administra-tion appeared to be dictating, there would be problems. On the other hand, if the administration took a passive, noncommital stance, there would also be problems.

It was becoming evident that a change in the existing seven-period schedule was needed if we were to have a significant impact on student learning. Exactly what that change would look like was anyone's guess at this juncture.

DATA COLLECTION

KEY QUESTIONS

- ◆ What data is available that is directly related to the problem or opportunity being considered?

- ◆ Does the data establish a discrepancy between what is and what should be?

- ◆ Is the discrepancy significant enough to warrant the intervention?

- ◆ Has the data been summarized in a way that can be understood by a variety of audiences?

- ◆ Does the data analysis serve as the basis for developing an action plan?

The discussions of the planning team began to deal with the more substantive issues of how well the existing curriculum was aligned with the newly adopted curriculum frameworks and for the future of MHS students. It was noted that the number of MHS students who planned to pursue postsecondary education had continued to rise over the years from a rate of 60% of the graduating class to the present rate of 80%. Although things appeared to work well for some students, we had to consider whether the existing schedule was preparing all students for the future. One of the concerns generated by the shift to an information and knowledge-based economy is whether a new caste system will be created. The information and knowledge-based economy is an evolving system that is based on the access to information and a resulting change in values. As we become more technologically dependent, information and knowledge could separate our society into an elite class and an underclass. If this occurs, we should also recognize that a society dichotomized by ignorance and knowledge will not share the same values. Therefore, unless schools can guarantee each individual equal access to information as a basis for knowledge, such a dichotomized society may become a reality. We were committed to avoiding such a dichotomy for students at MHS.

At MHS, the inequities of the existing schedule did not provide all students with the same opportunities. We also had to reflect on the state-mandated curriculum frameworks and the standards, contained within the frameworks, that would serve as the basis for the high-stakes testing program in the core curricular areas. The successful completion of these high-stake tests would be required of all students to earn a high school diploma. A review of MHS data indicated that students who matriculated in a program of studies that included four years of English, history and social sciences, mathematics, and science and technology scored substantially higher on standardized tests than students who engaged in three years of history and social sciences, mathematics, and science and technology (see Figure 1.3, p. 16). Similarly, students who enrolled in classes in those disciplines for three years scored substantially higher than students who only enrolled in such courses for two years. However, like most high schools in the area, the MHS graduation requirements only required students to successfully complete two years of history and social studies, mathematics, and science and technology classes in addition to four years of English. While world languages were recommended, especially for the college preparatory program, there was no world languages graduation requirement. Consequently, academic achievement in the core academic disciplines varied greatly among graduates because their exposure to the core curriculum varied greatly. Students completed their respective programs of study from a wide variety of courses in the various disciplines, including the core curricular areas. However, as Figure 1.1 (p. 8) indicates, most students also were placed in study halls for at least one period per day in the daily schedule that existed during the 1995-96 school year.

While we were analyzing the needs of students at MHS, the state university and college system raised the eligibility standards for student acceptance in terms of course work in the core curricular areas, GPA, and standardized test scores. As a result, we recognized that the MHS graduation requirements, outlined in Figure 1.4 (p. 17), and curricular standards would have to change if our students were to be successful in terms of their academic and career goals. Although the existing seven-period day schedule could have accommodated the increased requirements of the core curriculum, there would have been ancillary consequences. The elective programs and the variety of courses that were available to enrich student learning would suffer. Basically, if you increased the mandates in the core curricular areas from two to four years, increased the recommended number of years of successful completion of a world language from two to three years, maintained a four-year physical education requirement, and introduced a fine arts and practical arts requirement, then there would be less time for the elective courses outlined in Figure 1.4. Ideally, we wanted to both increase our requirements in the core curriculum and maintain our elective programs.

FIGURE 1.3. SAT SCORES:
DISAGGREGATED BY YEARS OF CORE CURRICULUM AND CLASS

English, History, Math, & Science	Class of 1994		
	Verbal	Math	Total
4 yrs	537	515	1052
3 yrs	511	492	1003
2 yrs	410	410	820
Mean	520	505	1026

English, History, Math, & Science	Class of 1995		
	Verbal	Math	Total
4 yrs	547	535	1082
3 yrs	485	484	969
2 yrs	395	402	787
Mean	523	515	1038

English, History, Math, & Science	Class of 1996		
	Verbal	Math	Total
4 yrs	527	517	1044
3 yrs	481	464	945
2 yrs	436	437	873
Mean	508	500	1008

FIGURE 1.4. 1995-96 GRADUATION REQUIREMENTS: SCOPE AND SEQUENCE OF CURRICULUM

Period	Freshman Year	Sophomore Year	Junior Year	Senior Year
1	English	English	English	English
2	History	History	Elective	Elective
3	Mathematics	Mathematics	Elective	Elective
4	Science	Science	Elective	Elective
5	W. Lang. or Elective	W. Lang. or Elective	Elective	Elective
6	Study	Study	Study	Study
7	P.E./Health/Read	P.E./Health	P.E./Study	P.E./Study

All of the key stakeholder groups recognized that changes would have to occur if MHS was to fully comply with state mandates, address the recommendations of the NEASC evaluation report, and address the needs of all students at MHS. The stakes were high, but we had to look at the available data. There were numerous programmatic inequities as well as inequities of opportunity for students within the existing MHS structure and curriculum. The curriculum was weighted heavily to meet the needs of approximately half of the student population and only marginally so for the remainder of the students. There were the new state curriculum frameworks that established standards for the achievement of all students, with which MHS had to comply. There were immediate and long-term recommendations set forth by the NEASC, which MHS would have to meet to maintain its accreditation. There were test data that indicated that students' academic achievement could be improved with curricular changes. There were existing MHS graduation requirements, which, if minimally met, would not allow a MHS graduate to meet the new eligibility requirements for the Massachusetts state university and college system.

All of this information was readily available to each stakeholder group and generally understood by each group. However, more often than not, this information was reviewed in isolation rather than from a holistic perspective (i.e., test data was generally reviewed as test data, with little or no relation to other aspects of the teaching and learning process). When the data was favorable, they were warmly received with appropriate accolades and back patting. When the data was less than favorable, there were the usual cries for improvement and initiatives to do better were undertaken. However, these public disclosures and pledges rarely impacted the classroom because they generally did not involve teachers directly. Somehow we had forgotten, or perhaps never fully recognized, that Thomas Edison didn't develop the light bulb by improving on a candle. If we were to meet all of the mandates to improve the academic achievement of all students, then we were had to do more than tinker with the existing system. We had to make fundamental changes at MHS.

RULES, ROLES, RELATIONSHIPS, AND RESPONSIBILITIES

KEY QUESTIONS

- ◆ What are the key rules that govern the operation of the school?
- ◆ What are the demographic factors that will need to be considered at the school setting?
- ◆ What are the key organizational characteristics of the school?
- ◆ What are the key elements and working relationships within the school's culture?
- ◆ How are decisions made at the school level?
- ◆ Have the duties and responsibilities for implementing the intervention been determined?
- ◆ Are the responsibilities within the sphere of influence of the people who will be assigned a particular task?

Recognizing the need for change and developing a plan for change in a school requires the efforts of people at all levels of the school department. At MHS, it required an examination of where we were within the organization, where we wanted to go to meet our fundamental purpose and expectations, where we needed to go to meet the various mandates that were being imposed, who would be responsible for developing and implementing the various changes, and how we could successfully complete our goals. It was from these perspectives that we began reviewing the existing rules, roles, relationships, and responsibilities within the Milford School Department.

The rules at MHS, as in any organization, were the formal policies, those that were written and formally adopted, and the informal policies, those that governed the way things got done. The policies that governed activities and actions from the school department level down to the classroom level ranged from the written policies in districtwide policy handbooks and the district contractual agreements to the adopted policies that governed activities at an individual school. At the school level, these formal policies governing MHS were generally reviewed annually as part of such documents as the student-parent handbook and the program of studies. There were also the informal policies established at the school level that generally governed procedural activities such as which rooms would go to which lunch, which rooms would exit through which doors in a school evacuation plan, when and how certain school activities would take place, and so forth. If we were going to make changes in the normal school day schedule, we decided that such changes would require changes in both the formal and the informal rules that governed MHS. However, from a contractual point of view, the structure and operation of the school day at that time was considered a management function. Teachers were guaranteed a duty-free 30-minute lunch period and a preparation period, but the time of the preparation period was not specified. This was a major stumbling block in the contractual negotiations that occurred during the 1997-98 school year.

Most of the rules in effect at MHS had remained basically unchanged for a number of years. So, too, had the faculty. The vast majority of the faculty had been at MHS for more than 20 years. The age of most of the faculty ranged from the late 40s to the late 50s. They comprised a veteran faculty, many of whom had graduated from MHS, that had experienced few changes during their careers and were now, in many instances, more focused on retirement than on accepting the challenges that lay ahead. But, they had their honor and genuinely wanted to help their students to learn and to succeed.

While the faculty had remained stable, the student body reflected changes that were occurring in school districts across the country. Increased mobility within our society had led to an increasingly diverse student body. For some faculty members this was troubling. Things weren't the way they use to be. Instructional and behavioral techniques that had "worked" for years were no longer as effective as they had been. As a result there was a sense that although some things were changing at MHS, there was also the hope that many important aspects of MHS would remain unchanged.

While the rules governed the actions of people, it was their respective roles, both formal and informal, that defined the way individuals acted and functioned within the system and at MHS. Implicit in the roles was the expectations for action by the individuals occupying a given position in the school department as they dealt with other people. The roles at MHS were both positional and situational (i.e., some individual administrators and teachers functioned differently in different situations). Therefore, we recognized that we could not just rely on the positional duties and responsibilities of any one individual or group of individuals to accomplish a particular task. We needed to look for the formal and the informal leadership characteristics among individuals. There were a number of individuals who were oriented to complete a given task, some who possessed outstanding organizational skills, others who possessed problem-solving skills, still others who possessed good written and oral communication skills, and those whose interpersonal skills allowed them to interact with a variety of constituencies. Although many of these individuals were held in high regard and respected within the school, they did not hold a leadership position. Our task was to enlist the support and energies of all individuals to achieve our vision for a new MHS.

Getting things done within the system at MHS required people to interact with one another through a variety of formal and informal relationships. These relationships were the key to the interpersonal interactions that produced outcomes within the system and at MHS. As a result, we had to examine the variety of social relationships that existed at MHS. If we were to bring about change at MHS, we had to expect that one person's behavior would elicit a dependable and expected response from another person. The extent to which similar responses tended to follow particular requests was one indicator of the effectiveness of the relationship. If we were to create an atmosphere of change, we needed to reflect upon the various relationships that existed within MHS between individuals and between groups of individuals.

The relationships among the various populations at MHS were normal for a high school. The relationship between faculty and the student body was positive. The faculty supported students, and the students generally liked their teachers. There were few incidents where students were disruptive in class. Similarly, the relationship among students was also positive. Relatively few incidents of discord among the student body were observed, and the relationship between the administration and the student body could be classified as very positive.

From the perspective of the change process that would need to occur, the relationship between the administration and the faculty was professional in nature. Teachers generally viewed the new administration team as supportive, although there was some question of how effective they could be within the bureaucracy of the Milford School Department. Because there had been little direction or supervision by the administration, there was little or no feeling of collegiality between the faculty and school administration. However, if there was a fly in the ointment of harmony, it was among the members of the faculty. Although the faculty was fiercely territorial in terms of their respective disciplines, their interpersonal relations were cordial at best. Within some disciplines relationships ranged from professional tolerance to open hostility. Generally, the various disciplines tended to be collections of individual teachers who had remained relatively unchanged by their professional relationships, rather than a collegial group whose interactions produced synergistic results. Thus the overall culture of MHS could be classified as cordial, but not collegial.

Within this setting, the decision-making process had tended to follow the traditional top-down, bureaucratic model. However, the state reform efforts had given considerably more authority and autonomy to individual schools to enact reforms. This was not universally accepted at the various bureaucratic levels, because it was the intent of the state reform to vest the operations of the schools, including personnel decisions, at the school-site level. This meant that a new set of relationships was being established at the very time when the knowledge of how things got done was a primary concern of the new MHS administration.

An understanding of the established relationships within a school and a school system indicates what one might expect when implementing an intervention. However, as the TEAM (Together Everyone Achieves More) proceeds, there is also a need to consider the responsibilities of individuals. Responsibility—the ability to choose a response, to answer for ones actions or decisions—empowers people to act. One of the major criticisms of education by the general public is the lack of accountability of educators. This may be the result of the traditional hierarchical structure of schools in which the top-down micromanagement that frequently occurs limits the authority of principals and teachers to respond in many situations. This combination of rules, roles, and relationships at MHS formed the basis of the culture at MHS.

The culture of a society is a historically rooted, socially transmitted set of deep patterns of thinking and ways of acting that give meaning to human experience. These patterns unconsciously dictated how experience was seen, assessed, and acted on. The culture of MHS described the character of the town as it reflected the beliefs, values, and traditions that formed over a period of time. Essentially, MHS was a microcosm of the expectations that the town had for its children. After all, the Milford public schools were the institutions by which the town created the conditions for its perpetuation. A former blue-collar mill town, Milford had a long history of supporting youth activities and its schools. In Milford, as in most small New England towns, the roots of the community were deep and the culture was very provincial. Residents of the town could be classified into two groups—Milford-ians and carpetbaggers. As a result, the winds of change did not readily blow through the halls of MHS.

Since the publication of Silberman's *Crisis in the Classroom* (1970), to the more recent reports of the 1980s that followed the National Commission on Excellence in Education's *A Nation at Risk* (1983), to the various state led reform efforts of the 1990s, the various stakeholders in the educational process—business leaders, community members, parents, and educators—have called for educational reform, particularly at the high school level. Furthermore, the ability to design high schools so that the reforms are long lasting is very much within the competency of the current professional personnel and within the range of present fiscal resources. However, the question remains as to whether these individuals and the communities they serve have the desire, leadership, persistence, and creativity—the sheer passion—to really challenge the change process and develop a different kind of high school that will serve *all* students.

REVIEW OF THE RESEARCH

KEY QUESTIONS

- ◆ Does professional literature exist that is related to the problem setting or the opportunity at hand?
- ◆ Has someone answered the questions or implemented the intervention being considered?
- ◆ What were the results or experiences?
- ◆ What questions have been generated to guide the research?

As we prepared for the responsibilities associated with the changes that we would propose for MHS, we needed to be reasonably sure that the approaches and methods we were contemplating would lead to the development of a sound action plan. Therefore, before we presented our concepts for MHS to the various stakeholder groups, we reviewed the literature relating to school improvement. The purpose was to learn whether someone had already answered the questions or implemented aspects of a plan that we might be interested in, what their experiences had been, and to inform and help us crystallize our views on a variety of topics associated with the alignment of curriculum, the teaching and learning process, and the organization of the normal school day.

We expected that opponents of our plan would be armed with and ready to present information from various sources, so we wanted to know and understand the information that was available, both pro and con, and why something worked or did not work in a given situation. Gathering this information ultimately proved beneficial to our efforts.

Prior to beginning our literature review we generated a series of questions about problems and opportunities at MHS to act as a guide for our inquiry. We knew that we would have to meet the requirements established by the state, to address the recommendations of the NEASC, and to develop a means of moving MHS from a school based on the industrial assembly-line model to a school that prepared all students to meet the highly skilled needs of the twenty-first century. How could we keep the best of the past and present, while moving MHS toward a new vision of academic achievement for all students? How could we expand our requirements for all students in the core academic disciplines while maintaining our rich elective offerings? How could we improve student learning in all disciplines? How could we assist teachers to improve instruction? How could we establish student-centered classrooms? How could we assess the effectiveness of our action plan? How could we eliminate all study halls and still be fiscally responsible? What would the school schedule look like in such a school? We felt that knowing the answers to these questions would help with the implementation of a plan to address our problems and our opportunities. However, there were too many questions, so we narrowed our focus to the delivery of the curriculum within the parameters of the normal school year and the normal school day.

One of the primary means of reforming high schools across the country was the implementation of block scheduling. As we searched for applicable literature, we also contacted colleagues from across the state, the region, and the nation with regard to our questions and block scheduling. Although we found plenty of favorable comments from colleagues and in the literature regarding block scheduling, we did not just focus our efforts on this trendy innovation. We expanded our literature review beyond educational journals, to domains such as business, psychology, and sociology regarding organizational change and the process of learning. We read books, we read reviews, and we looked at secondary sources, primary sources, and research journals. We also recognized that as we reviewed the literature and as we spoke with colleagues, we would need to transform their interventions, interpret their findings, and transform their recommendations into a format that would be both personal and site-specific to MHS.

Our initial research indicated that the development and implementation of the block scheduling concept in high schools across Massachusetts and across the nation did not necessarily mean the same thing in various communities. Furthermore, we discovered that block scheduling was not a new concept, was actually a generic term for a variety of models, was being implemented for a number of different reasons, and was meeting with a great deal of resistance in some communities.

At MHS, block scheduling had been in effect for a number of years on a limited basis (i.e., some science classes had laboratory periods, once per cycle, that were double the length of the normal classroom period and some advanced classes in practical arts also met on a daily basis for a "double" period). These classes met for 90-minute periods to allow students to engage in hands-on classroom experiences. Similarly, students who attended the area technical and career centers experienced classes that were regularly scheduled for time periods of 90–120 minutes. At MHS, however, this was not the case in most of the core academic areas or in disciplines where a considerable amount of time was lost preparing for classroom activities (such as the fine arts and physical education).

Although there were areas of the country where block scheduling had been used for some time, there was only one Massachusetts school that had implemented this form of scheduling for more than a few years. From a historical perspective, block scheduling had been implemented in one Massachusetts public high school after the 1982 passage of the Massachusetts taxpayer initiative called "Proposition $2\frac{1}{2}$" that had dramatically restricted local funding for all municipal services, including education. This block scheduling initiative, known as the Copernican Plan, was implemented to achieve a goal of reducing the number of faculty members at that particular school while maintaining curricular and programmatic integrity. This perspective was utilized during the development of the MHS action plan by opponents of the plan as a means of frightening key stakeholder groups.

Although block scheduling was not a new concept, it was a new concept to many high schools. More precisely, the concept of block scheduling actually referred to any form of scheduling where one or more of the periods of the normal school day extended beyond the normal time allotted for a class on the high school level (i.e., beyond 45–55 minutes per class). Generally, there were three basic models in general use in high schools across the country (see Figures 1.5–1.7). However, within the various communities that have adopted one of the following models there are a great number of variations to meet local priorities. In addition, each model has aspects which proponents feel are beneficial in achieving the particular goals of their respective school, and some limitations. Basically, these models reconfigure the traditional six- or seven-period school day by doubling the length of time a student spends in each class per day. Figure 1.5 illustrates the transformation of a traditional six-period school day into an alternate day or AB block-scheduling model. Each student enrolls in six courses per year, but attends only three classes per day. Each class lasts for approximately one-third of the school day *or* for one extended learning time (ELT) period. In this model, and in hybrids of this model, each course meets on alternating days for the entire year. The idea of longer periods of time being reserved for instruction in a particular discipline is common on the elementary, middle school and postsecondary levels. Ironically, it is the high school —the link between the adolescent and the adult life of the individual students we serve—that is the most rigid, the most controlling, and the most stifling to the creativity of successive generations of students.

FIGURE 1.5. BASIC AB MODEL OF EXTENDED LEARNING TIME (ELT)

Alternate Day Schedule—AB Model (6 Courses)

Days		A Monday	B Tuesday	A Wednesday	B Thursday	A Friday	B Monday
P E R I O D	ELT 1	1	2	1	2	1	2
		1	2	1	2	1	2
	ELT 2	3	4	3	4	3	4
		3	4	3	4	3	4
	ELT 3	5	6	5	6	5	6
		5	6	5	6	5	6

Many districts adopted a block-scheduling model so that they could increase the number of courses that a student could enroll in during a school year. This is especially true for those districts that have a seven-period day and desire to move to a block-scheduling model. Either Figure 1.5 or Figure 1.6 could be used to achieve such a goal. In Figure 1.5, the alternate-day model readily accommodates eight courses per year with four classes meeting every other day for an entire school year. In the 4x4 model of Figure 1.6, the primary difference is that each class meets daily during an ELT period for only one semester of the school year. At the close of the fall semester, students enroll in four entirely different courses. Although students enroll in eight courses per year in both models, there are fundamental philosophical differences between the AB model and the 4x4 model. Nonetheless, these models both present opportunities for student engagement that traditional high school schedules cannot accommodate.

FIGURE 1.6. BASIC 4x4 EXTENDED LEARNING TIME MODEL (ELT)

Basic 4x4 Extended Learning Time Model (ELT) (8 Courses)			
Days		Fall Semester	Spring Semester
P E R I O D	ELT 1	Course 1	Course 5
	ELT 2	Course 2	Course 6
	ELT 3	Course 3	Course 7
	ELT 4	Course 4	Course 8

Figure 1.7 illustrates the basic trimester model of block scheduling. In this model, students spend a greater amount of time engaged in a particular course on a daily basis, but for a fewer number of days during the school year. Students enroll in six courses per year, and each course meets daily during an ELT period for one trimester per year.

FIGURE 1.7. BASIC TRIMESTER MODEL OF EXTENDED LEARNING TIME (ELT)

Basic Trimester Model (6 Courses)			
	Trimester 1 (60 Days)	Trimester 2 (60 days)	Trimester 3 (60 days)
Morning (ELT)	Course 1	Course 3	Course 5
	Lunch	Lunch	Lunch
Afternoon (ELT)	Course 2	Course 4	Course 6

Not only were there a variety of block scheduling models, they were also being implemented for a number of different reasons. In some cases, schools were utilizing a block scheduling model to meet the requirements of state-imposed reform mandates. Still other schools were looking to increase the number of years that all students were required to spend in the core academic areas, while maintaining their existing programs. By expanding the course offerings on a yearly basis from six or seven courses per year to eight courses per year, schools could increase the requirements in the core curricular areas and maintain local initiatives. Essentially, much of the movement toward the adoption of block scheduling was being driven by educationally sound practices, whether the initiative for such practices was locally adopted or mandated by state.

MHS faced similar problems and opportunities. However, our problems focused on the curriculum and the resources to implement increased curriculum mandates while maintaining locally established curricular programs. Nonetheless, the traditional seven-period day would have allowed MHS to meet the new requirements, but it did not address the delivery of the curriculum nor the impact on students (see Figure 1.8, p. 28).

In this organizational pattern, students meet for 46-minute periods per day (with the exception of the lunch period that meets for 57 minutes) and 999 hours of directed instruction per year. To implement this schedule requires the addition of 13 to 14 full-time teachers to the MHS faculty (see Figure 1.2, p. 12). It also requires that resources be provided for the new classes (i.e., textbooks, supplies, materials, and equipment). However, with the addition of requirements to each of the core discipline areas, our established elective program would be somewhat adversely affected. Figure 1.9 (p. 29) highlights the positive and negative aspects of the plan from a curricular perspective and from a student and teacher perspective.

In prior years, students at MHS were discouraged from enrolling in seven periods of classes per day because of the implications for staffing. As a result, although the normal school day had seven periods, most students engaged in five courses plus physical education per year. The addition of two courses to a student's schedule would have been a dramatic increase in the number of classes that students were required to prepare for on a daily basis. Therefore, we decided to look at a six-period day, which would add, on average, only one course to a student's schedule per day (see Figure 1.10, p. 30). This was not a radical option, but rather one that had its roots in the traditional core curriculum prior to the 1960s and the infusion of elective courses in the various disciplines in the comprehensive high school. Although MHS had diversified curricular offerings, this option needed to be

FIGURE 1.8. TRADITIONAL 7-PERIOD DAY AT MHS

Period		7–Period Day			
		Freshman	Sophomore	Junior	Senior
Period 1 7:50–8:36		English	English	English	English
Period 2 8:39–9:25		History	History	History	History
Period 3 9:28–10:14		Mathematics	Mathematics	Mathematics	Mathematics
Period 4 10:17–11:03	Lunch	Science	Science	Science	Science
Period 5 11:06–12:33	11:03–11:33 11:33–12:03 12:03–12:33	W. Language	W. Language	W. Language	Elective
Period 6 12:36– 1:22		Fine Arts or Practical Arts	Fine Arts or Practical Arts	Elective	Elective
Period 7 1:25–2:11		P.E./ Health	P.E./ Health	P.E./ Elective	P.E./ Elective

explored because it offered the least impact upon the scarce resources needed to implement the increased requirements in the core curricular areas.

In this organizational pattern, students meet for five 55- minute periods plus a 57-minute lunch period per day, or 996 hours of directed instruction per year. However, because there is no time available for students to elect a course in the practical arts (business education, trade and industry, or family and consumer science), the potential exists for the elimination of the practical arts programs and the teachers who taught those programs. Although there would be an increase in students in each of the core disciplines, which students could select, would be dramatically curtailed. The net result could be additional reductions in the teaching staff in the core disciplines. The fine arts is another area that could be adversely impacted. This schedule would dramatically limit students who were interested in the per-

FIGURE 1.9. TRADITIONAL 7-PERIOD DAY AT MHS—PROS AND CONS

Pros	Cons
• Meets ERA "Time on Learning" mandates • Provides for elective program • The schedule was familiar to teachers	• No laboratory periods will be scheduled • Teachers will prepare for 5 classes/day • Students will prepare for 7 classes/day • Teachers will meet an average of 100–125 students/day • Students will meet with 7 teachers per day • There are 7 transitions per day for students • Requires the addition of 10–11 teachers *or* increases class size of 4–5 students/class • No homeroom period • Requires additional textbooks, supplies, materials, and equipment

forming arts. On the positive side, fewer offerings would result in a more balanced distribution of students in the various sections of the master schedule and fewer demands for textbooks, supplies, materials and equipment. Figure 1.11 (p. 30) highlights the pros and cons of this organizational pattern.

Both the seven-period and six-period day would have a profound impact on students. First, it became obvious that maintaining the traditional seven-period day was not a means of maintaining the status quo. In fact, maintaining such an organizational structure was the most costly option that was considered in terms of both personnel and classroom supplies (i.e., textbooks, supplies, materials, and equipment). It was the most familiar to teachers and students, but not with the elimination of study halls. Under the new format, students would have to prepare for seven different classes, seven different sets of teacher expectations, and homework for more classes than they had experienced previously. Second, the six-period day would save valuable resources. However, although there would be more hours available for the core curricular areas, the cost in terms of the curriculum options for students precluded serious consideration of that format. Therefore,

FIGURE 1.10. TRADITIONAL 6-PERIOD DAY AT MHS

Period		6–Period Day			
		Freshman	Sophomore	Junior	Senior
Period 1 7:50–8:45		English	English	English	English
Period 2 8:48–9:43		History	History	History	History
Period 3 9:46–10:41	Lunch	Mathematics	Mathematics	Mathematics	Mathematics
Period 4 10:44–12:14	10:44–11:14 11:14–11:44 11:44–12:14	Science	Science	Science	Science
Period 5 12:17–1:12		W. Language	W. Language	W. Language	Elective
Period 6 1:15–2:10		P.E./ Health	P.E./ Health	P.E./ Fine Arts	P.E./ Fine Arts

FIGURE 1.11. 6-PERIOD DAY AT MHS—PROS AND CONS

Pros	Cons
• Meets ERA "Time on Learning" mandates • Facilitates better balancing of class size • Laboratory periods can be scheduled for all classes • Provides 30 additional hours of instruction in each of the core disciplines	• Teachers will prepare for 5 classes/day • Students will prepare for 6 classes/day • Teachers will meet an average of 100–125 students/day • Students will meet with 6 teachers per day • There are 6 transitions per day for students • Eliminate the practical arts programs • Eliminate 9 teachers • No homeroom period • Eliminate most elective programs • Reduction of 1 course/year

our attention was drawn to some form of ELT scheduling that appeared to have more positive than negative characteristics. Figure 1.12 illustrates a 4x4 or an AB ELT model that incorporates the MHS curricular priorities and goals.

FIGURE 1.12. 4x4 OR AB ELT SCHEDULE AT MHS

Semester or Day A and B		4–Period Day			
		Freshman	*Sophomore*	*Junior*	*Senior*
Period 1 7:50–9:13		History	History	English	English
Period 2 9:23–10:46	*Homeroom* 9:16–10:20	Science	Science	Mathematics	Mathematics
Period 3 10:49–12:44	10:49–11:19 11:31–12:01 12:14–12:44	P.E./ Health	W. Language	P.E./ Fine Arts	P.E./ Fine Arts
Period 4 12:47–2:10		Elective	Elective	Elective	Elective
Period 1 7:50–9:13		English	English	History	History
Period 2 9:23–10:46	*Homeroom* 9:16–10:20	Mathematics	Mathematics	Science	Science
Period 3 10:49–12:44	10:49–11:19 11:31–12:01 12:14–12:44	W. Language	P.E./ Health	W. Language	Elective
Period 4 12:47–2:10		Elective	Elective	Elective	Elective

In this organizational pattern, students meet for four 83- minute periods per day and 996 hours of directed instruction per year. However, the structure is the most radical in terms of teacher acceptance. Although there are a number of attractive aspects in this option for teachers, teachers worry about what and how they would teach in an ELT environment. While this option requires additional resources, it also provides more curricular and instructional benefits than the other options. Figure 1.13 outlines the positive and negative aspects of an ELT schedule for MHS.

FIGURE 1.13. 4x4 OR AB ELT SCHEDULE AT MHS—PROS AND CONS

Pros	Cons
• Meets ERA "Time on Learning" mandates • Provides for elective program • Laboratory periods can be scheduled for all classes • Teachers will prepare for 3 classes/day • Students will prepare for 4 classes/day • Teachers will meet an average of 50–60 students/day • Students will meet with 3 teachers/day • There will be 3 transitions/day for students • Addition of 1 course/year	• Reduces the time for each class by 13.5 hrs • Requires the addition of 5–6 additional teachers • Requires a comprehensive professional development program for teachers • Requires additional textbooks, supplies, materials, and equipment

Finally, although more and more schools looked to develop and implement block scheduling at the high school level, they faced increasing resistance in some communities. This resistance generally came from the more conservative members of two key stakeholder groups—teachers and some parents of high-achieving students. Generally, as a group teachers tended to resist any substantive changes in schools, while the parents of students who were at or near the top of their respective classes tended to worry about a change in the organization of a system that seemingly is working well for their son or daughter. In most cases, it was a practical example of "the devil you know is better than the devil you don't know."

Regardless of the model that different schools used, the experiences and the empirical results obtained in schools that implemented block scheduling tended to be similar. Using a set of common indicators of school based performance, these results were obtained in most schools:

♦ Student grades in classes tended to improve;

♦ Student daily attendance tended to improve;

♦ The number of students achieving at an honors level tended to increase;

+ Student failures in courses tended to decrease;
+ Student disciplinary referrals tended to decrease.

However, there did not appear to be any significant change in norm-referenced tests (e.g., SAT scores and state testing scores), although where changes were observed over the course of a few years the movement tended to be positive. These latter data were often countered by opponents of block scheduling by citing the "Canadian studies" (Batesman, 1990; Rafael, Wahlstrom, & McLean, 1986; Rafael & Wahlstrom, 1986) even though these studies were conducted at schools whose models were not analogous to most of the models being implemented in Massachusetts and across the nation. Furthermore, it was not surprising that the Canadian systems that were studied experienced difficulty with student achievement and retention of learning. Therefore, it was important that we were able to counter the claims of opponents with the research findings and the data that we had obtained that was specific to our action plan model.

DEVELOPING THE ACTION PLAN

KEY QUESTIONS

+ What are the key areas of change that will occur during the implementation of the plan?
+ What are the potential approaches, strategies, or interventions for the plan?
+ What are the arguments for the implementation of the plan?
+ Have the fiscal, human, and social capital necessary to implement the plan been identified?
+ Are the various resources that have been identified realistic in terms of the plan and the school?
+ Will the various resources be available to implement the plan?

During the development of our action plan and during the implementation phase of the block scheduling model at MHS, our thinking changed considerably. At the outset, our review of the literature focused on block scheduling. It soon became evident that there was a small segment of the faculty and a number of parents who formed a coalition to oppose any movement toward block scheduling at MHS. As we were preparing our action plan, it became evident that speaking about block scheduling did not equate with the primary purpose and expectations of the school. Block scheduling did not address students, teachers, or teaching and learning; it was a nonpersonal organizational system. We then discussed the implications for students if we were to adopt an "extended instructional time" (EIT) model for the normal school day. This was an attempt to tie the non-personal organizational plan of block scheduling to the teaching and learning process. This approach persisted for a while. Much later in our discussions, we decided that the EIT approach focused on teaching when we were attempting to implement a model that focused on the student. At this point, we changed our focus from EIT to "extended learning time" (ELT). After all, what we wanted to accomplish was improved student learning and achievement. We also found that our opponents were much more reluctant to attack the ELT concept, preferring to refer to our initiative as "block scheduling."

We decided that developing and implementing some form of ELT had the potential to serve as the vehicle to move MHS toward a new vision of academic achievement for all students. An ELT model could help us to keep the best of the past and present, while expanding our requirements for all students in the core academic disciplines; to maintain our rich elective offerings; to improve student learning in all disciplines; to assist teachers to improve instruction; to establish student-centered classrooms; to align the MHS curriculum with the Massachusetts curriculum frameworks in each discipline; and, to eliminate all study halls and still be fiscally responsible. Exactly which model would be adopted required input from the various stakeholder groups, extensive professional development for the MHS faculty, the fiscal resources to adequately implement the plan, the establishment of a timetable to implement the plan, and the development of a plan to assess the effectiveness of our program.

Our initial approach included the development of a plan to be presented, in the order indicated, to the MHS faculty and staff, the MHS student council, the MHS Council (an advisory group composed of an equal number of students, parents, teachers, and community members, plus the principal), and the central administration for review, recommendations for improvement, and, ultimately, endorsement. The central component of our initial proposal was a 4x4 ELT model (see Figure 1.6, p. 26). After presenting our plan to the various stakeholder groups, it was our intent to present it to the Milford School Committee for its review and to hold publicized public forums for direct community input into the plan. This approach was followed and valuable input was received from each of the stakeholder groups and from the public forums, which resulted in positive modifications being made to our plan. Although this process delayed the implementation of the plan for one school year, it allowed us to develop and implement a comprehensive professional development program (discussed in Chapter 2) that was one of the primary keys to the success of our efforts.

As noted earlier, the existing seven-period day (see Figures 1.1, p. 8, and 1.8, p. 28) allowed MHS to meet the time-on- learning mandates of the Massachusetts Education Reform Act of 1993 (ERA). In addition to these mandates, the proposed model would allow us to meet the scope and sequence in each of the core curricular areas (see Figure 1.14) and increase our graduation requirements in each of the core disciplines in our effort to improve student achievement across the curriculum. Under this plan, we could increase the total number of courses that students could enroll in during their tenure at MHS, while reducing the number of classes a student and teacher had to prepare for daily. In addition, we could provide equity in terms of the length of the periods and the establishment of time for hands-on laboratory experiences for all students in all classes. These desired outcomes could be achieved merely by changing the structure and organization of the normal school day schedule.

FIGURE 1.14. PROPOSED GRADUATION REQUIREMENTS: SCOPE AND SEQUENCE OF CURRICULUM

Period	Freshman Year	Sophomore Year	Junior Year	Senior Year
1	English	English	English	English
2	History	History	History	History
3	Mathematics	Mathematics	Mathematics	Mathematics
4	Science	Science	Science	Science
5	World Language	World Language	World Language	Elective
6	Fine Arts	Practical Arts	Elective	Elective
7	P.E./Health/Read	P.E./Health	P.E./Elective	P.E./Elective
8	Elective	Elective	Elective	Elective

Although we felt that organizationally we could accomplish our ends, we needed to enlist the support of the faculty before implementing our plan. We recognized that fundamentally education is about changes in what a person knows and is able to do—it is a people process. Therefore, we presented our initial proposal to the faculty as a "win-win proposition." We explained how we could meet the goal of increasing our requirements in each of the core disciplines as well as many of the NEASC recommendations, reduce the number of classes and the number of students that individual teachers would teach on a daily basis, and eliminate study halls.

From a policymaking perspective, we could achieve these results and maintain our average class size with the addition of six full-time teachers. It would have taken the addition of 14 full-time teachers to maintain the existing average class size if we had maintained the 7-period day (see Figure 1.2, p. 12). The reasoning behind this projection was the shift in the manner in which time during the normal school day was allocated over the course of a year. Although teachers would only teach three classes per day, they would essentially be teaching six classes per year as opposed to the five classes per year that they were teaching during the 1995-96 school year. Furthermore, although each teacher was dealing with an average of 100–125 students per year in the 7-period day, under the new plan they would be dealing with 120–150 students per year. Hence, this was a "win-win proposition" for both teachers and policymakers. Because policymakers are always interested in the impact that any new proposal will have on students, we pointed out that students would also benefit by preparing for only four classes per day.

While the teachers felt that the rationale for the plan was sound, they did voice a strong concern for how they would deal with an ELT period of 83 minutes. Most of the veteran faculty had become accustomed to the 45–50-minute classroom break in the assembly line pattern of schooling. All they had to do in that brief interlude was to get the class of 20–25 students settled, adjust the mindset of the students to the new frequency of the discipline they were teaching, review homework, cover some new sound bites of information, check for understanding, bring the class to closure, and assign homework before the lesson was punctured by the sound of a bell so that the assembly line could start moving again. If that sounds hectic, it was. Now, consider how difficult it would be for a teacher to give every student in the class one minute of individualized attention and accomplish all the tasks required of them. It was little wonder that they were concerned. However, we explained that we would convey to the policymakers that we would not endorse the implementation of the plan unless it was adopted with a strong commitment to a comprehensive professional development plan for the faculty.

Not only were additional faculty members and a commitment to a comprehensive professional development plan necessary for the implementation of the action plan, but the 1,300 to 1,400 study-hall students who would be moving from a study hall into classrooms would need the normal textbooks, supplies, materials, and equipment for the classes. At an average cost of $40 to $50 per textbook at the high school level, the fiscal resources for this aspect of our plan were considerable when compared with previous budget allocations.

When the MHS faculty endorsed the ELT action plan, they did so with a number of reservations. The faculty felt certain that the additional faculty members, the professional development plan, and the additional classroom resources would not be made available to them. However, perhaps even more important to the individual teacher was the concern regarding the 83-minute ELT period. There was also the question of whether or not we should adopt the proposed 4x4 ELT model or some other form of ELT. With these concerns in mind, we informed the faculty that, where possible, common planning time would be established for teachers within a particular core discipline to facilitate discussions among faculty members. This was not always feasible (e.g., it was not feasible to shutdown the gymnasium, a computer laboratory, the art facilities, a science laboratory, and so forth, without adversely affecting the students and class size). Therefore, common planning time was made available to English language arts, history and social sciences, mathematics, and world languages teachers during the 1996-97 and 1997-98 school years.

While numerous hybrids of both the basic 4x4 model and the basic AB model were reported to the faculty, the English language arts and history and social sciences departments were strongly in favor of the 4x4 model for the personalization aspects of working with small numbers of students during a single semester that such a model would provide. On the other hand, the mathematics and world languages departments favored the AB model for continuity in the developmental process of their respective disciplines. The remaining disciplines were not as philosophically tied to either model.

After more than a semester of debate, visitations, and consultations with teachers who had experienced both models, the mathematics department endorsed the 4x4 model at the close of the 1995-96 school year. The math teachers reasoned that a semester model would allow students to complete a greater number of sequential courses at the high school level. Students would no longer be restricted by the level of mathematics they had mastered prior to entering high school. The world language department went along with this plan, with reservations, even though students would be able to reach higher levels in a world language with a semester schedule. At this point, we had the endorsement of the faculty to proceed with our action plan. It was interesting to note that the plan was not unanimously endorsed by the faculty, but rather by a consensus of the faculty. If an actual vote had been taken, the faculty endorsement might have ranged from a simple majority to a 60–40 majority. In politics, this might have been considered a landslide, but to reform a high school this was not a mandate. Neither the MHS Council nor the MHS Student Council, both of whom endorsed our action plan, expressed these same reservations.

What made this process interesting was the suggestion by some members of the faculty that the administration make the decision and issue a mandate to the faculty. To others, the fact that the new administration did not issue a mandate was an indication that the administration was unwilling to make a decision. For the majority of the faculty, they welcomed the input into the decision-making process. To the small group of faculty members who were opposed to any form of ELT scheduling, empowering the faculty gave them time to enlist the support of people outside the school to mount a campaign to defeat the action plan. As Machiavelli observed, this group of dissidents was vicious and tenacious in their attacks; in their overt and covert tactics; in their use of truths, half-truths, and untruths; and in their disregard for data and research that supported any position other than their own. When confronted or when their tactics were exposed, there was almost a sense of pride in their exclamation, "Welcome to Milford!" Fortunately, this was not the dominant sentiment within MHS, the school department, or the community, which was more interested in improving the schools than in the defeat of our action plan.

As the decision-making process continued, it became evident that the full ELT component of our action plan would not be implemented during the 1996-97 academic school year. Nonetheless, the Milford School Committee did recognize that there would be a need for additional faculty members at MHS. Over the course of two school years, it supported and allocated funds to hire six additional teachers. In addition, it enthusiastically endorsed and funded an ongoing and comprehensive professional development plan for the MHS faculty and staff. The Committee also indicated that it was prepared to provide the fiscal resources for the necessary textbooks, supplies, materials, and equipment, and for the upgrading of technology throughout MHS to make our action plan succeed. While this may sound as though we had a cakewalk, it should be noted that the MHS administration appeared at a vast majority of the public school committee meetings during the two years from December 1995 to December 1997. At these meetings, the administration would respond to questions from the committee and justify virtually every aspect and every detail of our plan. Finally, the Milford School Committee formally adopted a resolution to implement a 4x4 ELT model at MHS for the 1997-98 school year.

CONDITIONS FOR CHANGE

KEY QUESTIONS

- What is the history of successful change in the school department and at the school?
- How satisfied or dissatisfied are people with the present school operation?
- How compatible is the proposed intervention with existing and educationally sound practices?
- How many of the key stakeholder groups are likely to support the intervention?
- How many bureaucratic levels will be involved in implementing the intervention?
- How extensively has the intervention been communicated to the various stakeholder groups?

During the development of our plan to implement an ELT schedule, we detected a strong sense of reluctance to change on the part of the faculty and among a number of parents. Although there had not been any significant changes at MHS in more than a decade, it seemed that the history of changes that had been implemented at the elementary and middle school levels in recent years had left parents with a bitter taste. This sentiment was evident when parents expressed their concerns at public forums where we presented our plan to implement an ELT schedule. There was a feeling among these parents, particularly parents of students in the Class of 2000, that their children were again going to be "guinea pigs" for an educational innovation without any guarantees that the plan would prove to be successful for all students. Even though there was a realization that things would have to change because of the state-mandated reforms and the recommendations of the NEASC evaluation report, there was a feeling that the conditions for change were not favorable.

There was a general consensus among all of the key stakeholder groups that MHS was a pretty good high school. While MHS did have its share of the normal concerns that parents, teachers, and students express about most high schools, there was also the sentiment that one often hears when planning for change—"If it ain't broke, don't fix it." After all, the existing organizational structure of MHS was in place when many of the parents of MHS students graduated from MHS. Basically, for some people who were not familiar with all of the inequities and failings of the existing system or who did not experience them when they were students at MHS, and who were not familiar with the state mandates, there was a feeling that with a little tweaking here and a little tinkering there a new MHS would emerge. Therefore, to propose something as radical as the basic 4x4 ELT model was tantamount to throwing the baby out with the bath water.

Unlike many programs implemented in high schools across the country that target select populations, our plan would have an impact on every student and teacher at MHS. Yet we believed that we would be expanding the educational opportunities for all students and teachers alike, while maintaining most of the existing and educationally sound practices that had been in effect at MHS. We were also fortunate that our plan was ultimately developed with input from all of the various stakeholder groups and would be site specific. We would have to rely on the existing MHS administration, faculty, and staff to successfully implement our plan. However, because the Milford School Department was composed of only three elementary schools, two middle schools, and one high school serving approximately 4,000 students in grades K-12, we did not have to deal with the bureaucracy of larger school districts.

In finalizing our action plan, the administration, the faculty and staff, the student body, and the school council recognized the need for substantive changes if MHS was to prepare students to meet the challenges of the next millennium. They were prepared to accept the task of restructuring MHS for the future, even though the conditions for change were not favorable.

OPERATIONALIZING THE ACTION PLAN

KEY QUESTIONS

- ♦ Are the expected results described clearly?
- ♦ Are the approaches, strategies, and interventions clearly established and stated?
- ♦ Has a time frame for the implementation of the action plan been established and stated?
- ♦ Has a means of monitoring the progress of the action plan been established?
- ♦ Has a timeline been established to assess the impact of the intervention?

After much discussion and after listening to the concerns of students, teachers, parents and community members, a modified 4x4 ELT model was adopted for the 1997-98 school year at MHS. Accommodations were made to address the concerns relating to advanced placement (AP) courses, the performing arts program, the balancing of student schedules from semester to semester, the sequencing of courses, and the scheduling of English language arts and mathematics classes during the fall semester for senior transcripts. Basically, courses in each of the core disciplines were scheduled to meet daily for one semester. Most courses in disciplines such as the fine arts and the practical arts were scheduled to meet every other day for the full year, similar to the AB ELT model. However, some introductory courses in those disciplines met on an every-other-day schedule for a single semester, as did physical education and health. Figures 1.15 to 1.17 illustrate the typical student schedule at MHS.

Note that every attempt was made to schedule both English language arts and mathematics courses during the fall semester for seniors. To help balance student schedules, history and social science and science and technology classes were scheduled during the spring semester. Because many of the advanced level courses were composed of both junior and senior students, the typical junior and senior schedule looked very similar. Although Figure 1.9 (p. 29) does not indicate a world language, all students were required to earn 15 credits (i.e., the equivalent of three courses) in a world language other than English.

FIGURE 1.15. TYPICAL STUDENT SCHEDULE—SENIOR AND JUNIOR YEAR

Period Times		1997-98 Academic School Day Schedule			
		Fall Semester		Spring Semester	
		Day A	Day B	Day A	Day B
Period 1 7:50–9:13		English/Language Arts		Science & Technology	
Period 2 9:23–10:46	Homeroom 9:16–9:20	Mathematics		History & Social Sciences	
Period 3 10:49–12:44	10:49–11:19 11:31–12:01 12:14–12:44	Elective	P.E.	Elective	Elective
Period 4 12:47–2:10		Elective		Elective	

FIGURE 1.16. TYPICAL STUDENT SCHEDULE–SOPHOMORE YEAR

Period Times		1997-98 Academic School Day Schedule			
		Fall Semester		Spring Semester	
		Day A	Day B	Day A	Day B
Period 1 7:50–9:13		History & Social Sciences		English/Language Arts	
Period 2 9:23–10:46	Homeroom 9:16–9:20	Science & Technology		Mathematics	
Period 3 10:49–12:44	10:49–11:19 11:31–12:01 12:14–12:44	Elective	Elective	P.E.	Health 2
Period 4 12:47–2:10		World Language		Elective	

FIGURE 1.17. TYPICAL STUDENT SCHEDULE—FRESHMAN YEAR

Period Times		*1997-98 Academic School Day Schedule*			
		Fall Semester		*Spring Semester*	
		Day A	*Day B*	*Day A*	*Day B*
Period 1 *7:50–9:13*		History & Social Sciences		English/Language Arts	
Period 2 *9:23–10:46*	*Homeroom* *9:16–9:20*	Science & Technology		Mathematics	
Period 3 *10:49–12:44*	*10:49–11:19* *11:31–12:01* *12:14–12:44*	P.E.	Health 1 & Reading	World Language	
Period 4 *12:47–2:10*		Elective		Elective	Elective

The typical sophomore and freshman schedule (see Figures 1.10, p. 30, and 1.11, p. 30) had fewer electives because all sophomores were required totake Health 2, while freshmen were required to take Health 1 and Reading. Furthermore, most courses in the core areas were scheduled opposite the scheduling patterns established for seniors and juniors (i.e., English language arts and mathematics were scheduled during the spring semester). This reduced the number of different preparations that teachers had to plan for in each semester. Nonetheless, there was room in each of the four years for students to elect additional courses in any of the core disciplines or in the practical or fine arts.

Students who wanted to engage in the performing arts or the visual arts for four years were not restricted by this schedule. Similarly, students who wanted to explore courses in the practical arts had an opportunity to complete a four-year sequence of courses within this schedule. At the same time, all students who wanted to accelerate the sequencing of courses or to makeup classes that had been failed had an opportunity to engage in courses in the core disciplines during both the fall and the spring semesters. A number of students simply took additional courses in the core disciplines to supplement and enrich their respective program of studies.

The final piece in our model was the rotation of periods. As Figure 1.18 illustrates, three of the periods rotated, while the third period of the day did not rotate. There were two reasons for establishing such a schedule. First, some of the faculty members were itinerants (i.e., they taught a portion of the school day in schools other than MHS). Their schedules had to mesh with the times they were scheduled to be in other buildings. The second reason was equally as pragmatic and had to do with the lunch schedule. We wanted to provide as much uninterrupted class time as possible, to have an entire wing of the building eat during a particular lunch period, and, to the extent possible, balance the number of students eating during the various lunch periods. Because some classes met on an every-other-day or an AB model, the rotation illustrated in Figure 1.18 was established.

FIGURE 1.18. PERIOD ROTATION

Rotation	Day 1A	Day 2B	Day 4A	Day 1B	Day 2A	Day 4B
Period	1	2	4	1	2	4
Period	2	4	1	2	4	1
Period	3	3	3	3	3	3
Period	4	1	2	4	1	2

As you might expect, there was a great deal of interest in how well the ELT schedule was working. Weekly meetings were held with the action-planning team to review all aspects of ELT that could be thought of, and monthly reports were prepared for the central office administration and the school committee. Because of our sincere desire to make our ELT schedule work for students and teachers, we looked for the slightest problems. We wanted to make sure that small problems did not become large problems. We visited classes; we spoke with teachers and with students constantly. What were their reactions to ELT? We wanted to know if teachers were experiencing any difficulties. Were the textbooks, supplies and materials, and equipment adequate to meet the needs of each class? What did the teachers need in terms of ongoing professional development? We also wanted to know if teachers were teaching the adopted curriculum and if students were learning in the ELT classes.

To monitor the teaching and learning process, teachers actually began mapping the curriculum for each course they were teaching. They established what they wanted students to know and be able to do, what course content would be employed to achieve their objectives, a pacing guide was created, and they determined how they would assess student progress. This allowed them to align the MHS curriculum with the state curriculum frameworks in each discipline.

We had hoped that the ELT schedule would increase the options for students in all curricular disciplines, that students would become more active learners who would assume greater responsibility for their own learning, and that the learning environment would improve and be significantly less stressful for students. To assess the degree to which we were meeting our objectives, we planned to gather both quantitative and qualitative data. Our primary focus was on student achievement. Therefore, we gathered baseline data for the two years prior to the implementation of the ELT schedule. We looked at the levels of classes that students selected, student grades, grade retention, honor roll, student attendance, student suspension, and standardized test results. We also looked at class size data. From a qualitative perspective, we prepared surveys that allowed students, parents, and teachers to express their opinions on the success of the ELT schedule.

While most of the empirical data that we needed to make an assessment of the degree to which we were achieving our goals would not be available until the end of the 1997-98 school year, we would be able to gather some data at the end of each term. This initial information supported our projections that student achievement as assessed by course grades and student attendance improved, while disciplinary referrals declined. The superintendent of schools, who established a student advisory committee that reported directly to him, also conducted a survey of student opinion regarding the ELT schedule. This survey was developed and implemented in conjunction with the MHS principal. The results of the survey, which were overwhelmingly favorable, were then reported to the school committee and to the community. We were making a positive difference in student achievement as assessed by a number of quantitative and qualitative indicators, yet the opposition from a small group of teachers and parents continued despite the data we were collecting that indicated that the ELT schedule was having the desired effects on student learning.

SUMMARY

The process of developing and implementing an ELT schedule at any school is dependent upon a number of factors. The most important questions that need to be asked are What do you hope to accomplish and why? Once the goals are established, the process is one of:

♦ Gathering data that indicates that there is a difference between the empirical and the normative,

♦ Developing a plan that is well researched,

♦ Enlisting the support of key stakeholders,

♦ Preparing the stakeholders for the change process,

♦ Procuring the necessary resources to implement the plan,

♦ Putting the plan into action,

♦ Monitoring and making necessary adjustments to the intervention, and

♦ Reporting the results of the plan to all the key stakeholders.

While this appears to be a fairly simple process, our experience was that it required a great deal of perseverance and passion. What we have described in this chapter is a 2½-year journey filled with detours, potholes, roadblocks, and unmapped obstacles that would have made it easy for us to find a diplomatic means of maintaining some form of the status quo. However, when we weighed the potential benefits of an ELT schedule with our expressed goal of improving student learning, our decision to carry on was easy.

The details of our trials and tribulations, along with our celebrations, are described in more detail in subsequent chapters. Changing an American institution is no small task. Yet, if one considers that teaching is a group process but that learning is a process that takes place within the individual student, then transforming a traditional teacher-centered and content-driven high school into a learning center focused on students makes sense. Adopting an ELT schedule can help to achieve such an end.

2

DEVELOPING A COMPREHENSIVE PROFESSIONAL DEVELOPMENT PLAN TO SUPPORT EXTENDED LEARNING TIME

*The man who is too old to learn was probably
always too old to learn.*

Harry S. Haskins

Public secondary schools nationwide are dominated by veteran teaching staffs who have been delivering educational instruction using strategies and methods that have endured for many years in the standard 50 to 55-minute class period. With many states mandating educational reform, veteran teachers are being challenged to rethink the way they have been doing business for the past 20–25 years. New theories and empirical research relating to how students learn have caused many critics of education to call for organizational and instructional change. However, rather than jumping on the latest bandwagon, the key stakeholders in individual schools need to assess the need for change. They need to assess the alignment of the locally adopted purpose and expectations for schools with the organizational pattern and curriculum. The fundamental changes to the teaching and learning process occur in individual classrooms within the school. Therefore, in most cases where change is called for, changes in the behavior of individual teachers will be the key to the success of a new initiative.

When individuals consider changing the daily schedule of a school to promote a student-centered classroom and active learning, developing a

47

professional development plan that meets the needs of all teachers within a school is essential. In many schools, the change to some form of extended learning periods has been doomed from the start because the schools did not begin their initiatives with a comprehensive professional development plan. A worthy plan must evolve out of needs of the teachers and the school. Furthermore, the plan should not be mandated by the administration without teacher input. The success of any substantive reform or change process in any school district is linked directly to the professional development that accompanies the initiative. The investment that is made in preparing teachers for change will be directly related to the commitment of the teachers to the change process.

The importance of teacher involvement in identifying the needs of a school and the learning processes that will be utilized to address those needs is extremely important. Not only must individual needs be met, but they must be met within the context of the goals and objectives of the school. To achieve these ends, individual needs must be considered and must be organized around collaborative problem solving. This encourages both teachers and administrators to reflect upon and to evaluate the results of professional development initiatives. Whatever direction a school or district chooses, teachers must be involved in the decision-making process at the various stages of development and implementation of a new initiative.

Consideration should be given to creating a needs assessment team comprised of faculty from the different disciplines along with support staff and administrators. The composition of this team is critically important; all the disciplines should be represented. Involving the various disciplines in the decision-making process allows their concerns to be addressed during the process of developing a plan. It should be stressed to the individual members of the needs assessment team that remaining open-minded and willing to work toward the development of a program that addresses the expressed needs of all disciplines is in the best interest of the entire faculty and the student body.

Once the team is established, it can begin identifying needs and establishing professional development goals. If selecting a professional development team is difficult, then the needs of the faculty can be assessed via the school's existing hierarchical structure (i.e. department heads, team leaders, directors, or whatever liaison level exists between the administration and teachers). These individuals can consult with their constituents and work collaboratively to achieve the same end. Keep in mind that this process will not necessarily be smooth. Where opposition is encountered, the dissidents to this process are likely to be individuals who support the status quo and who are opposed to any form of substantive change in the school, especially an attempt to implement any form of extended learning time (ELT) scheduling. Dealing with these individuals is not easy, but they must be dealt with in a professional manner.

Because a new administrative team was the primary mover in the change process at MHS, we chose to make our department heads the members of our action-planning team so as not to appear to be undermining whatever authority, respect, and prestige the individual department heads had earned. Furthermore, because the department heads meet regularly with the members of their respective disciplines regarding curriculum, instruction, and assessment during contractually designated periods, we did not have to create additional after-school meetings. Another advantage of using this forum to collect data and information was the opportunity that teachers had to speak openly and freely with regard to their personal points of view.

The next step in our professional development needs assessment process was a timetable consistent with the school's plan for implementation of ELT. The school administration had the crucial task of presenting and defending a well-developed budget and impact statement to central administration and the school board. Therefore, both long- and short-term professional development initiatives had to be considered before the budget was presented.

Many schools have moved too fast with their schedule proposals and not included that part of the plan that is necessary to prepare teachers for the change. Teachers from such school districts have said that they felt like they were "thrown to the wolves." If teachers feel this way, imagine how students will feel and how classrooms will be impacted. To avoid these problems it is imperative that all of the questions involving teacher preparation be answered up front and be regarded with the highest possible priority.

We believed that the selection of professional development activities should occur simultaneously with all other aspects of researching the schedule best suited for MHS. However, the implementation of the professional development plan and a followup component needed to evolve before the ELT schedule was in place.

We kept track of the questions being posed during the discussions with the professional development assessment team. Because our focus was on improving student learning and achievement, we were pleased that these questions linked professional development and student success—a win-

win proposition. Some of the questions posed are discussed in the following paragraphs.

- Is the main reason for teachers to participate in professional development to increase their ability to help students to learn?

The answer should be obvious, but more often than not the question becomes, "What do the teachers need in order to survive in ELT scheduling?" With the focus on individual teachers, it often becomes personal. Many veteran teachers feel that they are being asked to completely abandon their chosen methods for delivering instruction, because these methods were never effective to begin with. One way to waste time, money, and effort is to give teachers this impression. We repeatedly stressed to teachers that our goal was to add to their existing instructional strategies rather than to eliminate their existing practices. They were reminded that today's students are expected not only to learn and become proficient in their respective disciplines, but also to learn how to become students of the learning process. We also asked them to consider that their students will need more than the ability to recall what they have learned, but will need the ability to find information when they need it and to use it to create new knowledge. Students will need to develop the ability to think critically and to work independently and cooperatively. The needs of society have changed; therefore, we need to modify our instructional strategies in the classroom. With this in mind, a fundamental shift in teacher thinking was required. Teachers need to think more about their students would be doing and less about what they have to do. Active learning requires teachers to stay focused on what student learning as the ultimate goal of their professional development activities.

- Will professional development activities be site-based and occur during the regular school day?

Teachers want to know how much of their time they will be asked to invest beyond the normal school hours. Therefore, we chose a variety of professional development activities that varied in length of time, the time of day when the activities were held, and so forth. By bringing professional development opportunities into the school during normal school hours, the a program's attractiveness to teachers was enhanced. Probably the most important aspect we added to our site-based professional development activities evolved out of "flexible scheduling." Specifically, "common planning periods" for most of the core disciplines were scheduled during the school day to allow teachers to work collaboratively.

With increasing concern for fiscal resources, student "time on learning," and the length of the school year when compared to other nations, an increasing number of school districts have eliminated early release days, which were used for professional development activities for teachers and staff. The loss of the early release days increased the importance of finding alternative strategies to provide site-based professional development activities during a variety of times, including normal school hours.

- ♦ Will the professional development plan have long-term goals in mind as well as a financial commitment from the central administration, the school board, and the school community?

When we presented the ELT scheduling plan to the policymaking body for approval, a long-term commitment to professional development was sought from that body. The assessment team developed a clear vision of what it believed teachers would need in the years following the implementation of ELT scheduling. These plans need to be flexible and are subject to change as needs are met and new needs identified. Nonetheless, considering both the short-term and the long-term implications of the professional development plan will make it more coherent and will allow you to project the fiscal resources that will be needed to implement the plan.

There were three major points to be considered in developing a plan. The first point was to invest in programs that the teachers felt were beneficial. Just because we felt that a program would meet the needs of teachers didn't mean the teachers will feel the same way. The second point was the selection of programs that provided useful and pertinent information that teachers could readily translate into teaching lessons for the classroom. While a theoretical perspective is always helpful to explain why a program has been developed, teachers consistently rated programs that provided them with the "nuts and bolts" that could be used in a classroom setting much higher than theory-based programs. The third, and perhaps the most important, point was the need to transfer information among faculty. This aspect of the plan was useful in assessing how well the resources were invested. It also helped to make the faculty accountable for taking what they had learned from professional development activities and shared the knowledge and skills with their colleagues. Using teachers to facilitate the sharing of instructional strategies, practices, and information among their colleagues over years made more sense than investing in the "itinerant preacher model" of professional development, where a preacher comes in for a day, preaches a good sermon, saves a few souls, and moves on. If we have learned anything with regarding to professional development, it is that the days of the "dog and pony show" as a one-shot cure are gone. We considered professional development without followup to be a form of educational malpractice. Both short-term and long-term goals need to be established.

♦ Will teachers assume responsibility for their own professional development by designing and directing professional development programs?

When the teachers were asked what they needed for professional development, they generally expressed their concerns and their fears regarding the ELT schedule. The thought of teaching in extended learning periods raised questions and concerns and evoked a number of emotions among members of the faculty. By listening to the teachers and giving them the opportunity to assist in the development of the plan that more specifically addressed their needs, worthwhile initiatives resulted. Keep in mind that ELT scheduling can be the cause of much anxiety, especially if teachers feel that they are excluded from the decision-making process. Unless this anxiety is tempered, the successful implementation of ELT scheduling could be a major problem. The teachers need to be involved every step of the way, especially in professional development planning. Teachers should determine what direction they want to move in. The administration should play a supportive and facilitative role, offering suggestions and helping keep the ball rolling.

♦ Will the professional development program accommodate the wide variety of faculty needs?

Many schools have jumped into ELT scheduling assuming that everyone on the faculty shares the same common need and requires the same basic training. This can be a costly assumption and can be avoided by enlisting the services of faculty leaders to collect data to identify specific faculty concerns and interests. By embracing this approach, we discovered that there were a number of issues that needed to be addressed. Initially, we found that while the faculty agreed that professional development was essential, they had a difficult time identifying what needed to be included in the professional development plan. The true nature of this dilemma became clearer when we listened to the concerns of individual teachers.

Some teachers told us that they have been using cooperative learning strategies in their classrooms since they started teaching and welcomed the opportunity to have more time to develop and foster group dynamics. Others told us that they had always relied on the lecture method and were confident that it was the best strategy for delivering instruction. Regardless of the variety and nature of the instructional strategies that were employed by individual teachers, we encouraged them to examine active student-centered teaching models. There were teachers who welcomed the opportunity to examine a variety of instructional strategies suitable for extended learning periods. Others made it clear that they wanted to spend their time with experienced teachers from other school districts who were utilizing an ELT model to gather materials and lessons for their classrooms. Some teachers responded well to professional development sessions that were conducted by educational consultants who attempted to bridge the gap between "theory" and "practical applications for the classroom," and there were teachers who felt that consultants were a waste of time and money. One of the most popular requests was for interdepartmental collaboration sessions where ideas can be shared and concerns aired among colleagues. Finally, there were teachers who continued to resist all professional development efforts, either by indifference or by their absence on the days when such activities were scheduled.

By offering the faculty a variety of opportunities for professional development, and by encouraging the teachers to make most of the decisions about their needs, we personalized the professional development initiatives as well as emphasized their importance. Those individuals who exhibited passive resistance were informed that they would be held accountable for the successful implementation of our ELT model, whether they chose to participate in the professional development activities or not. Nonetheless, we discovered that when the faculty "buys into" the professional development plan you can expect a return on your investment.

♦ How long will we have to prepare for ELT scheduling?

The amount of time needed to prepare for ELT scheduling depends on a number of factors (e.g., how great the difference is between the existing schedule and the proposed schedule; the variety of teaching strategies that individual teachers possess). As a rule of thumb, the more mature the faculty, the longer the curriculum has been in place without substantive revision, and the longer the existing schedule has been in place, the longer it will take for the faculty to feel comfortable with the impending change.

Although we spent a year preparing to implement an ELT schedule, it should not be assumed that "one year" is the magic formula to guarantee a faculty is ready for such a change. It is imperative that the teachers be involved in the development and implementation of the professional development plan. Some faculty members will feel ready at different stages of the development process, while others will not feel ready until they've actually completed the first semester or even the first year of teaching in extended learning periods. Establishing a target date to implement the ELT schedule and gauging how well the faculty is progressing in their readiness for the change is important.

There may be a few individuals who will never be ready simply because they choose not to be ready. Those individuals have to be given the utmost attention because their potential for distracting colleagues and slowing the process is immense. If they also happen to oppose the move to an ELT schedule, additional strategies may be needed to deal with them, especially if they decide to play by their own rules. In response to such individuals, we chose to counter their overt and covert actions by taking the moral high road. We enlisted the support of faculty leaders who welcomed the change efforts and who were willing to work with colleagues and students to keep the process moving forward. We were also careful when placing those individuals in group activities and we monitored those activities more closely.

Although the initial decision to move to an ELT schedule was reached by a consensus of the faculty, we did not feel that the decision was a fait accompli. After the decision was made, we expected that some general resistance would surface from the faculty when they realized that their decision would have a major impact on the entire student body and the faculty. We recognized that any major change process would bring with it some nostalgia for those teaching practices that seemed to be so successful for so many years. We began planning for those individuals who were eager to endorse the change process, for the large number of individuals who would take a wait and see approach to the change process, and for those individuals who would resist the change process once the implications for individuals became clear.

During this period, we identified the sources of the resistance and paid a great deal of attention to their concerns. If we were going to bring them on to the team, we would have to deal with their concerns while moving our vision toward reality. It was during this period that we decided that it would take at least one full school year to plan for the implementation of an ELT schedule.

THE FLOATING BLOCK

One of the first steps we took in moving toward an ELT schedule was the creation of a "floating block" within the normal school day. The existing seven-period day schedule did not rotate. This meant that each class period occurred at the same time each day. With the floating block we established

one 74-minute period, which moved from period to period with each suc-
ceeding day. The lunch period was 57 minutes and was the only period not
included in the 74-minute period in the rotation. This was also the period
when most of the itinerant teachers taught at MHS. To accommodate those
classes that met on an every-other-day basis, a separate cycle was added.
One cycle was designated as "red week" and the other as "white week," using the school colors to distinguish between the two cycles (see Figure 2.1).
Changing the rotation of the floating ELT during the "white week" ensured
that every class experienced the floating ELT, including those that met on
an every-other-day basis. Another benefit of the floating ELT was the establishment of a laboratory period for all science classes. Prior to the floating
block, only advance-level science classes had laboratory classes.

FIGURE 2.1. TRANSITIONAL SCHEDULE—THE FLOATING ELT"RED WEEK"

		1996-97 Academic School Day Schedule—"Red Week"					
		Day 1	*Day 2*	*Day 3*	*Day 4*	*Day 5*	*Day 6*
Period 1		**7:40** **8:54**	7:40 8:20	7:40 8:20	7:40 8:20	7:40 8:20	7:40 8:20
Period 2		8:57 9:37	**8:23** **9:37**	8:23 9:03	8:23 9:03	8:23 9:03	8:23 9:03
Period 3		9:40 10:20	9:40 10:20	**9:06** **10:20**	9:06 9:46	9:06 9:46	9:06 9:46
Period 4		10:23 11:03	10:23 11:03	10:23 11:03	**9:49** **11:03**	9:49 10:29	9:49 10:29
Period 5	*3 Lunches Times Varied*	11:06 12:36	11:06 12:36	11:06 12:36	11:06 12:36	10:32 12:02	10:32 12:02
Period 6		12:39 1:19	12:39 1:19	12:39 1:19	12:39 1:19	**12:05** **1:19**	12:05 12:45
Period 7		1:22 2:02	1:22 2:02	1:22 2:02	1:22 2:02	1:22 2:02	**12:48** **2:02**

("White Week" appears on the next page.)

FIGURE 2.1. TRANSITIONAL SCHEDULE—THE FLOATING ELT "WHITE WEEK"

		1996-97 Academic School Day Schedule—"White Week"					
		Day 1	Day 2	Day 3	Day 4	Day 5	Day 6
Period 1		7:40 8:20	*7:40 8:54*	7:40 8:20	7:40 8:20	7:40 8:20	7:40 8:20
Period 2		*8:23 9:37*	8:23 9:37	8:23 9:03	8:23 9:03	8:23 9:03	8:23 9:03
Period 3		9:40 10:20	9:40 10:20	9:06 9:46	*9:06 10:20*	9:06 9:46	9:06 9:46
Period 4		10:23 11:03	10:23 11:03	*9:49 11:03*	10:23 11:03	9:49 10:29	9:49 10:29
Period 5	3 Lunches Times Varied	11:06 12:36	11:06 12:36	11:06 12:36	11:06 12:36	10:32 12:02	10:32 12:02
Period 6		12:39 1:19	12:39 1:19	12:39 1:19	12:39 1:19	12:05 12:45	*12:05 1:19*
Period 7		1:22 2:02	1:22 2:02	1:22 2:02	1:22 2:02	*12:48 2:02*	1:22 2:02

Using this type of schedule prior to the full implementation of ELT scheduling had advantages for both teachers and students. Both teachers and students experienced extended learning periods by having one 74-minute class each day. Teachers had an opportunity to implement the different instructional strategies that they were adding to their repertoire through our professional development program on a daily basis in their classroom. The floating block gave teachers one full school year to practice and modify techniques, plan ELT lessons, and collaborate with colleagues.

Students also benefited by experiencing and meeting performance standards established for an ELT period. In turn, this helped the teachers fine-tune their instructional strategies and plan effective lessons for future ELT periods. At the same time, the administration encouraged teachers to experiment with alternative methods and offered support to those teachers who were having difficulties.

Perhaps the most important benefit of the "floating block" was that it gave teachers time to practice. The constant feedback teachers received from students provided them with a valuable and authentic assessment tool. The most obvious drawback of the floating ELT schedule was the time that was taken from the other periods to create the 74-minute period. As a result, teachers became even more frustrated with the issue of time, complaining of not having enough time to get things done in periods that were a few minutes shorter, but which approximated the length of the classes that they were accustomed to in the past.

Overall, the benefits of the "floating block" outweighed the drawbacks. It gave teachers a new perspective on what they could and what they could not accomplish in different periods of time. It also allowed teachers, students, and administrators to collect valuable data and information in preparation for the transition from a seven-period day to an ELT schedule at MHS.

- ♦ Will the interests and concerns of students be addressed in the professional development process?

It is ironic that the students, whose learning interests represent the primary reason for choosing a move to ELT scheduling, are often left out of the process completely, especially considering that the goal of a professional development plan is to help teachers modify instructional methods to better accommodate student needs. The students, as consumers of education, need to learn about the process and its objectives as much as the teachers. They had many of the same concerns regarding the curriculum and instructional strategies as their teachers. Furthermore, it is the students who will report to their parents how well or how poorly the ELT scheduling works.

Schools attempting to implement ELT scheduling could have difficulties or fail simply because they lost the "political" battle caused by not involving students in the process. Because there are many more students in the school than teachers, it is crucial that they be properly informed so that they can inform the rest of the community. Misinformation is a formidable enemy in any process. A misinformed student body will result in a misinformed community, which, in turn, can impact the decisions made by school boards and central administrations. Students have a lot more to lose than teachers if ELT scheduling becomes a reality before everyone is prepared for such a change in the school day.

Some teachers who oppose ELT scheduling may use the classroom setting to air their views and invite students to join their cause in scuttling the initiative. Some may be covert, using subtle innuendoes and planting seeds that will negatively impact student attitudes, while others may be more outspoken and overt in attempting to influence students. This can lead to confusion and a degree of anxiety among students regarding ELT scheduling. Be prepared to counter these tactics if faculty members use them.

There are a number of ways to get the student body involved in the process of learning about ELT scheduling. The most obvious method is to form a committee of student leaders that represents all grades and demographically diverse student groups. This committee can gather information related to student questions and concerns about ELT scheduling. The questions can then be brought to the action-planning team and the administration, who can to respond to questions and share other important information on the subject by addressing students in small groups or in large assemblies. As additional questions surface, there should be designated protocols and forums for collecting accurate information and responding to all concerned. Hold several meetings with the different grade levels or classes, the student leaders, the student council and small groups of students to explain your plan. Making students feel comfortable, involved and bringing their concerns to the faculty is a very important component of the process.

Sending groups of students to other schools that are using ELT scheduling is very useful to the change process because they can experience first-hand how an ELT-scheduled school operates. It is important that the schools students visit use a form of ELT scheduling similar to the one your school is considering, because different issues surround different ELT scheduling models. Visiting students should also have an opportunity to speak with both faculty members and students of the host school as well, as sit through at least a full day of ELT classes in as many different subject areas possible. The student visitation team should include members from all grades and have specific interests in mind. When they return, there should be a plan for disseminating the information that the students gathered from the visit to their classmates.

Student-faculty discussion forums can also prove beneficial because both students and teachers hear one another's concerns. More specifically, teachers who have relied heavily on expository methods of instruction need to hear students express their fear of 90-minute "death by lecture" sessions, and students need to hear teachers express their frustration over having to manage classrooms for extended periods with students who have short attention spans. These are just two of the many concerns that need to be aired when the lines of communication are opened. Useful dialogue will occur naturally, and students and teachers alike will continue to benefit from these discussions.

DEFINING PROFESSIONAL DEVELOPMENT OBJECTIVES

The first step in establishing the objectives for a professional development program is to determine what the needs are. Once the needs assessment is complete, planning activities designed to meet the objectives of the professional development plan can commence. It is important to state the objectives clearly because they will serve as the basis for evaluating the effectiveness of your program (see Figure 2.2). Another reason to clarify objectives is for accountability. With clearly developed objectives, compiling periodic reports for the school board and central administration throughout the year will allow them to review how the fiscal resources are being used, as well as how effective the activities are being perceived by the faculty.

FIGURE 2.2. MHS PROFESSIONAL DEVELOPMENT PLAN OBJECTIVES

MHS Professional Development Plan Objectives

- Provide faculty members with multiple opportunities to learn about new teaching strategies and methods for teaching in extended learning periods.
- Allow faculty members to have an active role in the selection of professional development activities.
- Use faculty members as facilitators to provide workshops and training for fellow faculty members in house.
- Schedule one extended teaching period (74 minutes) for each school day to give all the faculty members the opportunity to teach at least one ELT period each day for one school year.
- Create common planning periods for the core disciplines where members can work cooperatively to create a comprehensive program of studies.
- Provide faculty members with opportunities to learn about and implement curriculum development theories and practice.
- Provide faculty members with the opportunity to develop interdisciplinary curriculum units and courses.
- Expose faculty members to the multiple intelligence learning theory and strategies to address the needs of individual students in the classroom.
- Provide faculty members with the opportunity to learn from colleagues who are presently teaching in ELT periods.
- Provide faculty members with the opportunity to share with colleagues the information, knowledge and skills they develop from workshops, conferences and visits to other schools.

Stating objectives clearly and making them public knowledge from the onset of the professional development program will assist in keeping the program on schedule. There will of course be glitches and occasional bumps in the road that will require some modifications to the plan, but well thought out objectives help safeguard against scrapping the plan and starting over when unexpected problems surface.

All planned initiatives should be directed toward the achievement of the objectives and the expectations of all teachers. It is helpful to include an analysis of the expected number of hours the faculty will spend with the different activities, the overall goal of the plan in relation to the faculty, and the progress that the faculty is making toward achieve the goal. Figure 2.3 outlines the professional development objectives and procedures that served as a road map for the faculty and the administration at MHS in preparation for implementing an ELT schedule.

FIGURE 2.3. MHS PROFESSIONAL DEVELOPMENT PLAN TO DATE

Activity	Hours of Training Recommended	Hours of Training Required	Percentage of Faculty Completing Training
On-Site School Visits	6 Hours	0 Hours	70%
In-School Work-shops	18 Hours	18 Hours	100%
Graduate-Level Courses	36 Hours	0 Hours	50%
Application "Floating Block"	173 Hours	173 Hours	100%

In the spirit of collegiality, a series of guidelines and procedures were developed to foster the sharing of instructional strategies, procedures, techniques, and so forth, when the activities of a particular day were completed. By creating an atmosphere of sharing, the dividends for investing in people were compounded. Figure 2.4 outlines the procedures that were given to all MHS faculty members.

FIGURE 2.4. MHS PROFESSIONAL DEVELOPMENT PLAN PROCEDURES

MHS Professional Development Plan Procedures

♦ Departments choose courses, conferences, workshops, etc., that will meet the individual and collective needs of the discipline.
  • Department heads look to see that the fiscal resources are distributed equitably and that all members of their departments have the opportunity to get involved.
♦ Faculty members return from conferences, workshops, etc., and share with colleagues materials and information in the following manner:
  • Meet with department members during common planning periods,
  • Hold after-school sessions for larger groups of faculty where they are paid as facilitators and faculty are also compensated for service after school hours, and
  • Prepare workshops for small groups of faculty during in-service and contractual days.
♦ Faculty members visit schools and observe teachers teaching in ELT periods and follow the procedures outline for this type of activity.
♦ Specialists are brought to MHS to work with faculty in departments during in-school workshops who should then follow the procedures outline for this type of activity.

DEVELOP A DIRECTORY

It is important to identify those individuals who can best assist you in providing valuable information and resources for teachers preparing to teach in extended learning periods. By contacting area school districts that have implemented an ELT schedule, you can start collecting the names and references of educational consultants, innovative teachers, and other agencies that provide workshops and seminars for educators. State educational boards and administrator's associations are excellent sources for obtaining research data and references for current publications. The National Association of Secondary School Principals (NASSP) has generated a number of research activities on ELT scheduling, and the National Alliance of High Schools assists schools that seek to improve student learning and achievement.

The most important individuals in the research directory, however, will be teachers who have had success teaching in extended learning periods and are willing to share materials and information with educators from other schools. To teachers, colleagues are generally more credible and valued than consultants who, regardless of their expertise, are simply not classroom teachers. Once the directory has been established, be sure to share it with teachers and encourage them to make use of the resources.

SITE VISITS

Allowing teachers to visit area schools that have adopted ELT scheduling is a crucial professional development activity. However, there are a number considerations that need to be addressed so that teachers gain the maximum benefit from these visits. First, it is important to determine what will benefit the teachers the most during these visits. For example, will the teachers benefit most by spending their entire visit in classrooms observing extended learning lessons from start to finish, or by speaking to the students, faculty and administration of the host school? Perhaps a combination of classroom visits and informal question and answer sessions with members of the host school will be ideal in meeting the needs of teachers.

Once the a determination has been made of what will benefit the teachers the most, it is important to find host schools that can provide those benefits. Do not make any assumptions regarding what provisions will be made for the teachers while on a visitation. Schools that have the better ELT schedules are inundated with requests to host visiting teachers and have developed specific times and agendas for visiting teams, while other schools have just begun to host visitors and have not yet refined the process. There are schools that offer short orientation programs before dispersing visitors throughout their buildings and some offer guided tours. There are also schools that suffer from "host school burnout" and have lost their appeal as a visitor site.

If the ELT model that has been selected for a school is more of an issue than the long periods, it is important to send teachers to schools using the same or a similar schedule to the model that has been selected. Experience indicates that mixing models can create confusion and difficulties. For example, many of our teachers returned from visits to schools that had never considered the 4x4 model but which gave our teachers all of the reasons why the 4x4 semester plan wasn't a good option. Although these teachers had been party to the selection of the 4x4 model, they were now confused and wondered if they had made the correct decision. There are many reasons why different ELT scheduling options make better fits for different schools, and it is helpful to explain the differences in models to the faculty, especially if they are not a part of the team that will select the scheduling model for a particular school.

Once schools that can meet your needs are identified, determine how many teachers those schools can host during a visit, the specific subject areas that can be accommodated, and the daily itinerary that would be established for the teachers. This information can be made available to teachers along with directions to the host school well in advance of the visit.

Selecting the members of the visitation team will require a lot of thought and should begin by finding out how many teachers are interested in visiting other schools. Once this has been determined, the process of putting teams together and assigning them to one of the host schools can begin.

Keep in mind that the composition of visiting teams should include as many different individuals from as many different academic disciplines as possible. The support staff (i.e., guidance and adjustment counselors, special education teachers, media personnel, etc.) should not be overlooked because they are important members of the overall school team. Once the teams' visiting sites and dates are established, be sure that the composition of the teams is announced to the faculty so that they have a chance to meet and make plans.

Teachers on visiting teams often create their own car pools for their visits. This can be a valuable opportunity for faculty members to collaborate and, in some cases, to get to better know colleagues from whom they have been isolated due to the constraints of the existing schedule, the size of the building, and the traditional departmental structure of most high schools. Finally, faculty members returning from visits should report to other members of their departments as to their experience and answer any questions their colleagues might have.

Site visits to schools where students and faculty are excited about their new experience with ELT scheduling can be very uplifting and beneficial for your students and faculty. On the other hand, visits to schools that are not yet comfortable or confident with the process can create anxiety and doubt. Consider carefully which schools will be visited, for how long they have had an implemented ELT schedule, what their experience has been to date, what data and information they are willing to share, and how the faculty feels about the schedule. Figure 2.5 outlines sample procedures for teams making school visits.

FIGURE 2.5. PROCEDURES FOR SITE VISITS

Procedure for Site Visits

♦ Mark your calendars and develop a lesson plan for the substitute teacher on the day of your visit. Let your classes know in advance that they will be having a substitute and that you expect them to do the assigned work.

♦ Fill out a Professional Day form two weeks in advance and submit the completed form to the principal's secretary.

♦ Contact the other members of your visiting team and set up a car pool. Be sure to include the people you normally don't see in the building.

♦ Drivers should pick up directions from the office secretary a few days in advance of the visit along with predeveloped itineraries, if provided by the host school.

♦ Plan to leave in plenty of time to arrive on time for your visit.

♦ When you return, set up a time to meet with your respective department to share the information you received on your visit.

♦ Bring back any and all materials offered to you as well as names of consultants, workshop presenters or professional development programs different from our own.

♦ ENJOY YOUR VISIT!!!

IN-SCHOOL WORKSHOPS

One of the most effective professional development activities that we undertook involved developing customized one- day workshops for various academic disciplines. Faculty members were asked to meet with their respective department head to develop a workshop agenda for teaching strategies and instructional strategies for ELT classes. The agendas were developed to specifically address the needs and concerns of the faculty in their own curricular area. We then identified the best facilitator we could to further implement our professional development plan.

What was clear from the beginning of this initiative was the faculty's desire to have teachers in their respective specific disciplines to serve as facilitators for the workshops. Not only did they want colleagues, but they also wanted teachers that had at least a few years of experience teaching in an ELT schedule who would share information and materials. Teachers consistently noted that they wanted "hands on" materials, lessons for long ELT classes, group activities, and other classroom innovations that could be added to this new "bag of tricks" that they would need to teach in extended learning periods. Faculty members repeatedly emphasized that they did not want just "theory," research-based seminars, or discussion groups. They knew where they were headed—what they wanted was a road map to get there.

With the faculty taking ownership in the design and content of their workshop agendas, it was incumbent upon the planning team to find the facilitator best suited to their needs. There were a number of excellent teachers available who were excited about having the opportunity to share their materials with our teachers.

Remaining true to our goal of offering professional development activities on-site during school hours, the workshops were scheduled during the school year for six hours during the school day. This necessitated hiring substitute teachers for entire departments on workshop days, but with some creative scheduling it was possible to hire fewer substitutes than the actual number of teachers attending the workshops (e.g., combining a number of smaller classes and developing a common lesson). We had established a "substitute teacher process" for professional development days such as this. Figure 2.6 outlines a sample procedure for in-school workshops.

FIGURE 2.6. PROCEDURES FOR IN-SCHOOL WORKSHOPS

Procedure for In-School Workshops
Facilitated by Visiting Instructors

♦ Fill out a Professional Day form two weeks in advance and submit the completed form to principal's secretary.

♦ Prepare questions for your workshop presenter and give them to your department head. Questions will be forwarded to the workshop facilitator in advance of the workshop.

♦ Prepare your classes for your absence in advance and develop a lesson for the substitute teacher. Speak with other members of your department about consolidating your classes, where feasible. Work to develop collaborative lessons for the workshop day.

♦ Check with your department head one week in advance of your workshop to find out what time it will begin and end. While most workshops include six hours of meeting time, they do not all begin and end at the same time. Some of the facilitators will be traveling a long distance and will not be able to begin until 9:00 or 9:30, so it is possible that you may teach a class or two on the workshop date.

♦ Lunch will be provided with the compliments of the administration.

At the end of the individual workshops, teachers completed an evaluation, which included comments and recommendations for future professional development activities (see Figure 2.7). The following questions are from four core disciplines and were generated as part of the initial in-school workshops at MHS:

English Language Arts Workshop Questions

♦ What is eliminated from the curriculum and why?

♦ Are kids "grouped out" after working in groups all day?

♦ With fewer subjects per day do students actually spend more time on assignments? Can I assign 40 pages to read instead of 20?

♦ What is the policy concerning absences?

♦ Are there interim reports to parents other than report cards? If so, how are such reports handled?

♦ What is the policy concerning makeup work?

♦ How many different activities are needed to keep interest for 90 minutes? How many of these activities advance their learning or enhance the material being studied?

♦ Do you group according to ability?

♦ Do you often use activities for "fill" rather than start something new?

♦ Since all students must take English, a problem arises because the English teachers must, at times, play homeroom teacher and disseminator of information. Thus, are your English classes ever taken over or used for class meetings, etc., or do you have a "power block?"

♦ Do you have interaction with other departments? If so, how is this pulled off?

FIGURE 2.7. MHS WORKSHOP EVALUATION

MHS Workshop Evaluation					

Department: _____ Date: _____

Facilitator: _____

Excellent to Poor

1   2   3   4   5

1. Quality of Presentation

2. Applicable to Classroom Instruction

3. Useful and Beneficial for Lesson Planning

4. Sufficient Time to Cover Topics

5. Value as a Professional Development Activity

6. Quality of Materials Provided

7. Satisfaction with Answers to Questions

Comments:

History and Social Sciences Workshop Questions

- How can a teacher keep a class on task for an entire 85-minute period?
- What specific strategies, materials and plans can be utilized in an extended period?
- How successful can an extended period be when one has to also deal with multilevel grouping?
- What specific strategies can be implemented to keep multilevel students on track and focused during the extended teaching period?

♦ In your experience, why does the extended teaching period work for some and not for others? Does success depend upon attitude? Technique? Open-mindedness? Patience?

♦ How much workshop time and professional development, on average, does it take before the typical teacher feels comfortable with the extended ELT?

♦ What specific problems can we expect during the first year on the ELT schedule?

♦ How have you revised your social studies curriculum to meet the proposed curriculum frameworks? Which specific changes have you made to prepare students for the assessment tests?

♦ We are now concerned with the "big picture" of social studies and teaching our students to think critically on themes rather than just "memorizing" and "regurgitating" facts. From your experience, how does one get around the mere "covering" of material in order to focus more on the themes themselves?

♦ What do your U.S. history and world history curriculums focus on? In a semester course in U.S. history, how does one get from the colonial period through the 1990s in such a limited amount of time? How can one explore themes from ancient civilization through the present in world history in one semester? What is weeded out? What is the important focus?

Mathematics Workshop Questions

♦ What impact does the ELT have on curriculum content? Are topics eliminated or is it possible to discuss more than one topic in one class period?

♦ What specific changes in curriculum delivery have and have not been effective? We would like specific examples in courses ranging from prealgebra to calculus for all ability levels.

♦ Are the various teaching techniques sufficient to maintain student modification, especially at the lower-ability level?

♦ What are the methods of student assessment that can be implemented? How often are students tested and for how long? Are open-ended questions or projects incorporated?

- What hands-on activities and technology have been successfully utilized in various courses at all levels?
- Does the opportunity exist for interaction between the science and mathematics departments?
- How are appointments with guidance counselors and class meetings scheduled?

Science and Technology Workshop Questions

- How do microlabs increase efficiency?
- How much course content is omitted? Specifically, what topics are omitted in biology, chemistry, and physics?
- The longer period of time will benefit us in completing labs; can you describe for us a typical nonlab class day?
- How have you revised your science curriculum to meet the curriculum frameworks? What changes have you made to prepare students for assessment tests?
- Can you give us some examples of specific hands-on activities that work at various course levels?
- What computer applications have worked for you? Which specific programs?
- We are very concerned about keeping low-ability students motivated for 83-minutes everyday. How do you keep them motivated?

Prior to the full implementation of the ELT schedule at MHS, each of these questions was addressed. Some of the questions had definitive answers, some led to other questions, and still others helped guide the professional development plan. However, it was refreshing to note that the nature of the questions focused on curriculum and the teaching and learning process.

IN-SCHOOL TEACHER COLLABORATIVES

Once the move to ELT scheduling is underway and professional development initiatives have begun, it is time to plan for another important activity—the in-school collaborative. Teachers whose schools have moved to ELT scheduling indicate that one of the things they need the most is one of the things they get the least—time to collaborate with their colleagues. It should not be surprising that teachers request time to reflect on the impact that the professional development program has on their day-to-day teaching:

> We don't need another workshop or in-service session on multiple intelligences, learning styles, and cooperative grouping. What we need is time! We need time to plan lessons, rethink our curriculums and make decisions about course content. We need time to pool our resources and share our thoughts and concerns. We also need time to commiserate and renew our collegial relationships!

If this is a dominant teacher issue, why haven't more schools made this accommodation for their faculties. The answer may be simple or complex. Each school and school district has to find its own answer to this question. Experience does indicate, however, that good teachers will collaborate with colleagues if given the opportunity.

It seems ironic that teachers are asked to take on a major challenge that will force them to reorganize their classrooms and modify their teaching strategies and techniques, while they are not given the autonomy to decide how they want to do it. If teachers are expected to plan new lessons and re-assess old ones, they will need the time to plan, to reflect, and to evaluate their effectiveness in the ELT schedule. Furthermore, teachers are the key factors that will make or break the success of ELT scheduling. They must be trusted to do what needs to be done to make any schedule work for the students. After all, what other options do we have?

In-school collaboratives can take on many forms and occur at anytime during the school year. Interdepartmental group sessions provide an opportunity for members of a given discipline to work on course curriculum maps, pacing guides, portfolio assessments, course catalogues, and so forth. Collaboratives also provide an opportunity to discuss the pros and cons of teaching strategies as well as behavioral interventions and classroom management techniques.

Intradepartment collaboratives provide faculty members with the needed opportunity to discuss ELT scheduling issues with colleagues from other disciplines who they rarely see during the school year. The agendas for these meetings should be teacher-generated and include issues ranging from classroom management, to instructional strategies, to home-school communication, such as: student attendance and tardiness, makeup work, dealing with oppositional students, teaching inclusive and multilevel classes, communicating with parents, coping with classes of varying sizes, and getting groups to cooperate. Collaborative teamwork to resolve problems is a key process in a school improvement effort.

Teachers consistently relate that they gain valuable insight and often experience a morale boost when they get out from under the day-to-day routine to bond with "long-lost colleagues." When teacher morale improves, so does school climate, and a positive school climate results in improved student learning. Listen to your team leaders, department heads, head teachers, or whatever organizational structure is in place in your school; they may tell you that the faculty thinks that it might be a good idea to scrap the in-service agenda and use the time for collaboration. Some administrators may feel that this is a copout, believing that teachers will not use this time productively. However, given the opportunity, most faculties demonstrate that they are truly professionals.

Not all planned activities will be well received nor achieve the desired outcomes. For example, two in-service days with highly recommended educational consultants were planned for the MHS faculty. These consultants were highly recommended by schools that had implemented an ELT schedule. Based on faculty questions the focus of one session dealt with the process of change while the other session dealt with learning styles. Neither of these seminars was well received by the faculty who expressed frustration and concern over "wasted time." Although these sessions were warmly received in other schools, they met neither the needs nor the expectations of the MHS faculty. We listened to the faculty leaders and to the rank and file teachers and the followup sessions to these seminars were canceled.

The lesson to be learned is simple: nothing should be written in stone relating to the professional development process for ELT scheduling. Be open-minded, be flexible, and be willing to make changes and modifications that are in the best interest of the faculty. Stay focused on the goal of developing teacher ownership in determining what they need for professional development. Finally, make time for teachers to collaborate.

GRADUATE-LEVEL COURSES
FOR ELT SCHEDULING

Imagine a veteran teacher enrolling in a graduate-level course at a local college or university because the teacher was excited about what was being offered. Graduate courses nationwide, especially those in education, are considered by many teachers to be dull, time-consuming, general, and of little practical use. More importantly, teachers feel they are making an investment in something that will not necessarily translate into useful applications for their classrooms. Unless the teacher is enrolled in a degree program, chances are that the reason for taking a graduate course is either to earn credits to advance on the salary schedule or to fulfill requirements for recertification. The theory for enticing teachers to enroll in graduate-level courses is that the knowledge and skills that teachers gain will translate into improved student achievement. However, the majority of teachers are veterans who have attained the highest degree they aspire to or have reached their highest salary step. Furthermore, some schools are just too far away from graduate schools for teachers to commute and many school districts offer no course reimbursement or only minimal reimbursements for course tuition. Therefore, teachers need incentives when it comes to investing their own time for professional development activities.

Given these factors, a custom graduate-level course for ELT scheduling should be developed. If the development of such a course is undertaken by the school, a local state college or university may be more than willing to offer sponsorship. The next step is identifying someone who is willing to develop a course designed to meet the needs of the teachers and the school.

Once an instructor has been identified, it is time to map out the curriculum. The curriculum should be based upon identified best practices and evolve out of the teachers' needs. Therefore, as many members of the faculty as possible should be consulted. This is also a good opportunity to find out how many teachers would be interested in enrolling in such a course and what would be the most convenient time to schedule it. Most colleges require a minimum number of individuals to make the course feasible. Using the school as the site of the course increases the convenience for the teachers and may increase the number of teachers that participate.

Another matter to consider is tuition reimbursement. It may be possible to negotiate a tuition discount with the college or university. Furthermore, if the school district is committed to making the ELT schedule work and committed to the necessary professional development for teachers, then it might sponsor the tuition for such a course. In many districts that offer course reimbursement, teachers must first pay the tuition for the course and then provide proof that they successfully completed the course to receive reimbursement. As a commitment to the ELT schedule and the teachers, the Milford School Department paid the tuition for the teachers involved in locally developed graduate course upfront. This simple accommodation made an action statement about the importance of professional development and the need for teachers to get involved and resulted in greater teacher enrollment.

By the time the first course, "Curriculum Design and Teaching Methods for Extended Learning Periods," was completed, there were 20 satisfied and excited members of the MHS faculty. What they were most pleased about was the opportunity to share and collaborate with their colleagues and to spend their time developing lessons and innovations for their classrooms. They felt that it was time well spent and encouraged fellow faculty members to get involved. This lead to the development of a second course, which we offered during the next school year.

A site-based, graduate-level course that is tailored to meet the needs of your teachers, that prepares them to deal with the reality of ELT scheduling, that prepares them for their new ELT classes, that teaches them to collaborate with colleagues, that allows them to earn graduate credits, and that does not require them to pay for the course directly out of their pockets, can become the professional development initiative that brings it all together. Also, the successful experiences in the course will give teachers 40–45 hours of hands-on experience, as well as set the stage for creating future courses of this nature.

Figure 2.8 (pp. 74–76) outlines the syllabus for one such course. This course focused on delivering the adopted curriculum in an schedule, on increasing the instructional strategies of teachers, and on assessment techniques. Each of these themes was presented in a format that provided participants with the opportunity to develop materials, techniques, and strategies that could immediately be used in the "floating block." Furthermore, teachers had an opportunity to share their successes with colleagues and discuss those initiatives that were not as successful as they had hoped. Finally, this course was held from 2:30–6:30 p.m. for eight sessions. This intensive format allowed participants to model many of the strategies that we hoped teachers would use in an ELT schedule.

IN-SERVICE DAY WORKSHOPS

Although there has been an increase in the recognition that the professional development of teachers is essential to the improvement of the teaching and learning process, the means of delivering professional development activities conflicts with the need to increase student time-on-learning. As a result, many school districts are offering fewer in-service days for teachers. To counter this trend, the use of in-service days needs to be directed toward meeting the needs and expectations of both the school and the teachers.

(Text continues on page 77.)

FIGURE 2.8. GRADUATE-LEVEL COURSE DESIGNED FOR MHS FACULTY

Curriculum Design and Teaching Methods for Extended Learning Periods
Developed by John M. Brucato

♦ Objectives
  • To examine existing research and rationale for providing extended periods of learning time in the high school.
  • To explore workable models for managing learning time and student behaviors in extended learning periods.
  • To examine different teaching methods and instructional techniques suitable for extended learning periods.
  • To provide teachers with opportunities to develop lessons for extended learning periods, both individually and collaboratively.
  • To provide teachers with an opportunity to modify curriculum for extended learning periods.
  • To analyze the change process and the many issues involved in moving from 47- to 83-minute class periods.
♦ Content Syllabus
  • Session 1: Curriculum Planning and Instructional Design
    ▪ Instructional Design (Explanation, Application, Synthesis)
    ▪ Exploring a Variety of Teaching Models (Concept Development, Concept Attainment, Synectics and Memory Models)
    ▪ Preparing Lessons with Different Models
    ▪ Group Discussion: Modifying Teaching Models for Your Classroom
    ▪ Critique of Assigned Reading

  • Session 2: Designing Lessons for Extended Periods of Learning Using a Lesson Plan Template
    ▪ How to Plan the 90-Minute Lesson, Project-Based Learning, Problem-Centered Learning
    ▪ Critique of Assigned Reading

  • Session 3: Short Takes
    ▪ Interactive Strategies for Brisk Pacing, Providing Variety, and Ensuring Student Engagement with Content
    ▪ Critique of Assigned Reading

  • Session 4: Lecturing, Planning, and Direct Teaching
    ▪ Using Direct Instruction in the Lecture and in Planning
    ▪ Presenting New Material, Stating Objectives and Providing Guided Practice, Corrective Feedback, Independent Practice
    ▪ Group Work—Fine-Tuning Interactive Project

- Session 5: Cooperative Learning Models
  - Research on Cooperative Learning Practices
  - Managing Learning in Small Groups
  - Group Discussion: Getting Feedback on Group Composition, Student Roles, Learning Tasks and Assessment Strategies
  - Critique of Assigned Learning

- Session 6: Alternative Assessment Practices
  - Developing Task Criteria and Rubrics
  - Sample Rubrics and Rating Scales
  - Group Discussion: Getting Feedback on Tasks, Task Criteria, and Rating Scales (Rubrics)

- Session 7: Active Classroom
  - Simulations
  - Socratic Seminars
  - Learning Centers
  - Project-Based Learning
  - Problem-Centered Learning
  - Technology Integration
  - Group Work—Fine-Tuning Interactive Project

- Session 8: Individual and Group Presentations
  - Sharing Lessons and Individual Innovations
  - Question/Answer-Discussion
  - Critiques of Assigned Reading

♦ Description

The primary focus of this course is to give secondary school educators an opportunity to restructure curriculum and lessons for longer teaching periods and fewer class meetings. Course sessions include: alternative assessments for multiple intelligences, student-directed classroom methods, cooperative learning models, developing task criteria and rubrics, and interactive strategies for brisk pacing.

Teachers taking this course will have an opportunity to collaborate with colleagues to plan both intra- and cross-curricular lessons, share strategies, discuss concerns in the department, and develop usable lessons consistent with their new curriculum designs. It is expected that teachers will develop a better understanding of curriculum so as to keep "coverage" in perspective and that they will become comfortable in determining what content could and could not be omitted from the courses that they teach.

(Figure continues on next page.)

◆ Activities
  • Teachers will develop strategies for teaching in extended learning periods.
  • Teachers will develop lessons for extended learning periods.
  • Teachers will make decisions about what to include and what to omit in their individual curriculum.
  • Teachers will share ideas and strategies with colleagues.
  • Teachers will develop alternative assessment strategies.
  • Teachers will explore and examine multiple teaching models.

◆ Assignments
  • Teachers will be required to read a number of research articles, and to discuss and critique them.
  • Teachers will submit a pacing guide for a course that will be condensed from one whole year to a semester, or develop an outline for an integrated course or unit to be team planned with another teacher(s).
  • Teachers will develop a complete unit to be taught in a given semester, including specific class lessons with objectives, teaching methods to be used, breakdown of how time will be spent, and what assessments will be used to test for understanding.
  • Teachers will make a thorough presentation of their projects.

  Note: All qualifying projects must show evidence of collaborations in planning, implementing, and assessment of learning. The purpose of this project is to provide teachers an opportunity to document, apply, and reflect on strategies for effectively using longer ELT periods.

◆ Evaluation
  • Participants will be graded based on individual critiques of research material, active participation and presentations, and a final interactive project.

◆ Methodology
  • Teachers will spend class time analyzing research data, interacting with one another, and engaging in discussions. There will also be 8 to 10 hours of directed instruction, plus question and answer sessions involving a guest teacher who specializes in this area.

◆ Course Format
  • There will be *eight* intensive sessions of *four* hours each, and two independent study sessions (*eight* hours combined) wherein teachers will complete the development of and preparation for the presentation of their interactive projects.
  • Total contact hours will equal *forty* hours.

Many schools have made the mistake of hiring consultants for single-day agendas without informing them of the expectations and needs of the school and the teachers. As a result, they come to the school with a set of expectations that may or may not meet those of the school or the teachers. In the end, the faculty goes away with an opportunity missed and the consultants wonder what went wrong. In many instances, the teachers play a "passive" role of sitting and listening, when they want to be actively involved. Ironically, this is analogous to the position that students find themselves in on a daily basis. By choosing programs where teachers are engaged and given the opportunity to make contributions, the likelihood of favorable results increases dramatically. There are many issues involving ELT scheduling, far too many to be addressed during a few in-service days scheduled throughout the school year. Therefore, it is essential to establish priorities before committing to specific agendas.

Another option to consider is using in-service days to create a number of different opportunities and activities for faculty and staff to choose from. For example, some teachers can visit other schools; other teachers can work on curriculum with fellow department members. A visiting teacher could address teachers who have expressed an interest in a certain topic, and still another faction of teachers could meet with administrators to work on policies and procedures that will need revision in the current faculty and student-parent handbooks.

Regardless of what activities are offered, it is important to stay focused on faculty needs and not become overly ambitious with imposing agendas. Keep in mind that timing is essential. While there will be those days when it is crucial for everybody to get down to business, there will be those ideal times for faculty and staff to loosen up and laugh a little. No one said that teachers could not have fun while engaging in professional development activities.

We expected that after a couple of months of implementing ELT scheduling on a full-time basis, the faculty would be ready for some relief and for some time to commiserate with colleagues. Therefore, during the first in-service day of the new school year, we scheduled an individual who was quite popular and renown for his ability to make professionals laugh at themselves and the day-to-day occurrences that become the fodder of legend. He was especially skilled at getting teachers to focus on the reality of their circumstances, the importance of their job, and the humor in their daily lives. A student council appreciation luncheon followed this session, and the teachers spent the remainder of the day working on curriculum-related matters. The teachers appeared grateful for the opportunity to both lighten up and compare notes with colleagues while taking a mini-break from the rigors of ELT scheduling.

Another thing to consider for in-service day agendas is the development of activities for the support staff. When schools experience major changes such as ELT scheduling, few individuals feel the heat more than the secretaries, aides, custodial staff, and other individuals in the school. Many of these individuals will experience some stress with the new process. They need to know what is occurring and should not be neglected during the transformation to an ELT schedule. Whatever little it takes to include your support staff in the in-service agendas will be resources well spent.

SUBSTITUTE TEACHER PROCEDURES AND RESOLUTIONS

One of the most neglected but most important aspects of schools is the substitute teacher program. Most schools have procedures for substitute teachers to follow, as well as expectations for teachers when they are absent, but just how clear are they? For example, when a teacher is absent, is it the school's expectation that the curriculum continue or that students be given a study hall to be supervised by the substitute? Are the teachers held accountable for leaving well-developed lesson plans as well as updated class rosters and seating charts for substitutes? Do the students treat substitutes as counterfeit educators or are they cooperative? Do teachers take responsibility for the behavior of their students in their absence? Are substitute teachers well supervised and supported while in the building or are they left on their own?

Think of the specific questions that need to be addressed regarding substitute teachers and the implications for student learning before implementing ELT scheduling. First, prior to implementing an ELT schedule more teachers will be out of their classrooms while visiting other schools and attending seminars and workshops. This will bring more substitute teachers into the building. In turn, they will require both direction and empowerment to achieve positive results. It will not take long for the student body to determine what the school's posture is regarding substitutes, and they will have a picnic in their teacher's absence if the rules of decorum are not clear and enforced.

Second, when ELT scheduling becomes a reality in a school, the substitutes will be asked to supervise 85 to 90-minute classes. This is an important reason for substitute teacher training. If the regular teachers are anxious about dealing with difficult students for an ELT class, imagine how the substitute will feel. Also, with fewer class meetings per year per course, one of the natural outcomes of ELT scheduling, the consequences for student and teacher absences may be more pronounced than in a traditional schedule. Therefore, students need to complete assigned lessons that will be of value in the absence of their teachers. Changing student attitudes toward substitute teachers can only become a reality when teachers' attitudes toward substitute teachers change.

As a general rule, high school teachers have little faith in a substitute teacher's ability to teach their classes, and many concede that it will be a wasted day for their students when they are not there to teach them. If this is the prevailing attitude among the faculty, it will take some work to bring about the necessary changes that will allow substitute teachers to become effective teachers rather than mere supervisors.

All teachers need to assume responsibility for how their students behave in their absence by preparing meaningful lessons with clear instructions and well-defined performance standards. The lessons should contain enough content to keep students actively engaged for the entire ELT period and should include activities that students are familiar with. Making students accountable for completing the assigned work is as simple as having it collected by the substitute teacher and turned in to the regular teacher for review and evaluation. When students realize that the work that they do when their regular teacher is not present is meaningful and will become part of the normal assessment process, they will be less likely to take the day off or give the substitute teacher a difficult time. Similarly, the substitute teacher should have a clear understanding of both the general rules of the school and the individual teacher's classroom. In the event that the regular teacher does not have an opportunity to prepare for a sudden absence, they should have left in the hands of the school official responsible for scheduling the substitutes teachers a prepared "emergency lesson plan" and instructions for how it can be accessed.

Substitute teachers should prepare a daily report form for the teachers they replace and turn it in to the designated administrator or supervisor at the conclusion of the school day. This will allow the administrator to conference with the substitute teacher and give feedback to the returning teacher on the following day. The teacher, in turn, should complete a brief substitute teacher report upon returning. This system of checks and balances will make both the regular and the substitute teacher accountable for carrying out their responsibilities. It will also give the administration a better opportunity to place the proper substitute with the proper teacher. When all the parties recognize that the issue of substitute teachers is important to the administration, then the procedures and the process will become more important to all the parties.

Finally, a substitute teacher manual or "survival kit" containing all the most pertinent school policies and processes that they will need to know will be helpful. This manual should contain the essential school policies, expected student decorum, class schedules, bell schedules, discipline procedures, and so forth. These manuals should be provided for all first-time substitutes, along with a brief orientation by an administrator. The substitute teacher should be given an opportunity to review the contents of the substitute teacher kit prior to stepping in to a classroom.

INTERSCHOOL COLLABORATIVES

If there are a number other schools in the area that have adopted or that are anticipating adopting ELT scheduling, there are some interschool initiatives to consider. For example, with ELT scheduling, guidance counselors are challenged to rethink how they will service students, especially in schools where the new schedule has eliminated study halls. Counselors are faced with the tasks of pulling students out of academic classes and explaining the new schedule and options to parents and students. In addition, they need to be familiar with changing graduation requirements, procedures and policies, and a host of other details normally associated with guidance and counseling. It might be helpful for them to compare notes and share ideas with counselors from other schools.

With this in mind, we scheduled interschool collaborative sessions where individuals were invited to attend and share their practices with individuals from other schools. Although this is one example, interschool collaborations can be utilized in virtually any discipline or for any program and can address specific needs and concerns of individual disciplines. These collaboratives can also generate solutions to difficult problems.

Another interschool initiative that we undertook involved the creation of an ELT scheduling mentor team. The team was made up of individuals considered to be innovative in extended learning period classroom instruction. By contacting area school principals and asking them to nominate teachers for this team, a pool of educators who agreed to host visiting teachers from other schools who were interested in observing the mentor teachers' classes was established. A list of individuals who were nominated by individual principals or teachers was compiled and sent to interested school principals.

There are many advantages to developing an area mentor team. First, when a teacher leaves the building for a visit, the only cost involved is the hiring of a substitute. Second, the host teacher does not have any extra work to prepare or a need to modify the teaching schedule in any way. When a visiting teacher has the opportunity to observe a teacher from another school, he or she gains a much needed change of perspective as well as the potential for picking up useful teaching strategies, materials, and lessons. There are few risks to establishing such a program; and even if teachers initially do not take advantage of the opportunity to make visits, they will eventually see the value in interschool collaboration.

CREATING A PROFESSIONAL DEVELOPMENT BUDGET

A comprehensive professional development program does not necessarily have to be costly. In fact, there are a number of ways to keep costs down while achieving all of your objectives. We found that some of our most productive activities were the least expensive. For example, the honorarium for a visiting teacher to come to the school and work with all the teachers in a particular discipline plus the cost of substitute teachers came to far less than the cost of most of the workshop flyers that are routinely sent to schools. Furthermore, by sending faculty for site visits to area schools, the only cost incurred was the cost of substitute teachers.

Private consultants should be used where appropriate, but teachers generally prefer to hear from their colleagues. In addition, the fees of a consultant tend to be higher than the fees for teachers, but you can also check their references much easier than the references of a teacher. Consider the number of days that the consultants would be required and their fees when developing a professional development budget. If the programs of private firms, research institutes, or agencies are going to be used, take the time to contact the schools who have used them for references. Make sure that there is a component for followup by the people you hire as well as a post-program evaluation done by your teachers. Be sure that you have a clear understanding of what the consultants have to offer and that it is what the teachers want prior to making a commitment.

When investing in off-site workshops, conferences, and seminars, it is not necessary to send every member of a given department. Generally, this form of professional development works best when the goal is to make the teachers aware of a particular program or strategy. By sending two or three teachers with an understanding that they will make a scheduled presentation to their colleagues sometime after the conference is over, all interested members of a given department or faculty can benefit. When teachers get in the habit of sharing materials, ideas, and innovations with their colleagues, the school enjoys the benefits of many worthwhile programs for a few modest registration fees.

Finally, consider the cost of on-site graduate-level courses. If the school district offers tuition reimbursement for graduate-level courses, it is possible that the school district can negotiate a group tuition discount for developing an on-site graduate course about ELT scheduling. Even if the teachers are not reimbursed for tuition, it is still possible to negotiate tuition discounts with a state college. When you looking at the big picture, this may be a wise investment.

SUMMARY

Like schools that are committed to an ongoing professional development program, be prepared to offer the same development opportunities to teachers in the years following the implementation of an ELT schedule. When the ELT schedule is being implemented, teachers may not want to leave the building to attend workshops and seminars. In-school development programs are then very useful. What teachers may want, like many others who have moved to ELT scheduling, is more time to plan lessons and collaborate with colleagues. Providing this time is very beneficial to teachers and students. These initiatives cost little and set the stage for the planning of new programs. When professional development plans become the process by which a school addresses its needs and interests, stakeholders can be fairly certain that the outcome will meet those needs and interests.

3

QUESTIONS AND ANSWERS REGARDING EXTENDED LEARNING TIME

Here is Edward Bear, coming down stairs now, bump, bump, bump, on the back of his head, behind Christopher Robin. It is, as far as he knows, the only way of coming down stairs, but sometimes he feels that there really is another way, if only he could stop bumping for a moment and think of it.

A. A. Milne

Most changes that are implemented in a high school will have an impact, to one degree or another, on students and teachers. A change to an ELT schedule will have a profound impact on all students and teachers. As a result, a great number of questions will be generated, not only from students and teachers, but also from parents and other key stakeholder groups. Initially, the questions will tend to be open and honest. However, as a planning team begins to get serious about a proposed plan, more of the questions will tend to come from individuals and groups who are opposed to the plan. Regardless of the origin of the questions, be prepared and respond openly and honestly. Questions concerning the ELT model under consideration can assist in making modifications to the action plan that will ultimately benefit students. Because each ELT model should be developed so as to best meet the purpose, expectations, and needs of a particular school, questions from key stakeholders can draw attention to particular aspects of the plan that can be improved. Nonetheless, there are a number of questions that tend to be consistently asked regarding an ELT schedule.

The responses to the questions that follow are general and need to be customized to reflect your school and the ELT model under consideration. Keep in mind that simplistic and unqualified answers may not accurately portray the potential impact that an ELT schedule will have on the school, the students, the teachers, the curriculum, and a host of other factors. Thus, although the responses to the questions are presented from a generic perspective with specific reference to MHS and a review of the research regarding schools that have adopted an ELT schedule, there is a need to answer the question from the perspective of your school and its particular goals, objectives, and reasons for moving to an ELT schedule.

WILL TEACHERS BE ASKED TO TEACH MORE STUDENTS AND SPEND MORE TIME TEACHING EACH DAY IN AN ELT SCHEDULE?

The answer is—it depends on a number of factors. What does the schedule look like now, prior to the adoption of an ELT schedule, and what will it look like afterward? How many classes are teachers currently required to teach daily and how many will they be required to teach under the proposed schedule? How many actual minutes do teachers teach under the old format and how many minutes will they teach under the new format? How many students do teachers meet daily and over the course of a year now and how many will they meet with an ELT schedule? How many additional duties and responsibilities are teachers currently assigned and how many will they be assigned under the proposed schedule? How much preparation time do they have now and how much will they have under the new schedule? These are some of the questions that should be considered initially.

If the number of classes that students will enroll in during a semester or a school year is not increasing, then reducing the number of classes per day will also reduce the number of times that students will change classes during the course of a day. Because the school year for most students in the United States is 180 days, the rule of thumb is for each noninstructional minute you save, you will gain 3 hours per year of instructional time (i.e., 1 minute × 180 days = 180 minutes *or* 3 hours). Therefore, eliminating three classes from the daily class schedule also eliminates three passing periods per day. If each passing period was 4 minutes, the net gain in instruction time will be 36 hours per year (i.e., 3 passing periods × 4 minutes × 180 days = 2,160 minutes *or* 36 hours). Exactly how this time is used will be determined by the action plan and the ELT model that is adopted for a school. In most cases, at least a portion of the time, if not all of the time, will be apportioned among the remaining periods to extend the amount of time available for instruction and student learning.

IF TEACHERS MEET THEIR CLASSES FEWER TIMES, HOW WILL THEY BE ABLE TO COVER THE CONTENT OF EACH COURSE?

The question of coverage illustrates one of the key distinctions between teaching at both the elementary and middle school levels and the high school level. Elementary school teachers, and teachers who have adopted a middle school philosophy, teach students, while high school teachers teach content. This statement does not mean that elementary or middle school teachers are not concerned about the cognitive development of the knowledge and skills of students in the various disciplines, or that high school teachers are not concerned about the development of students as individuals. It does denote the differences in the perspectives from which teachers at the different levels of schooling approach the teaching and learning process.

Student learning is related to the amount of time available for learning and the variety and quality of the learning activities to which they experience. Figure 3.1 illustrates the relationship between the breadth of learning, the depth of learning, and time. Within the total amount of knowledge or "content" in a particular area, there is an essential amount of knowledge and skills that students must attain to successfully complete the adopted curriculum. There is also a certain amount of nonessential knowledge and skills that, if time were not a factor, would enrich and add detail to the learning of students. The basic question that needs to be addressed is whether to allocate time to "cover" more curricular content (i.e., the breadth of the curriculum) or to concentrate on the "depth" of learning.

Time is a resource that is both infinite (life-long learning) and finite (a school year) in terms of learning. Within the parameter of available time, teachers need to resolve the dilemma between the breadth of learning and the depth of learning. While they recognize that there is more content to be "covered" than there is time to "cover" it, they also recognize that not all content is created equal. Teachers can, and do so on a regular basis, decide what content is essential and most appropriate for their students. Hence, the taught curriculum constitutes the "breadth" of learning available to students in a given class. On the other hand, the "depth" of learning is directly related to the amount of time available for learning and the quality of the activities which students experience (see Figure 3.2).

There is a need for a certain amount of factual information and data to form a knowledge base. However, if coverage of the content becomes the primary focus of the classroom, student learning can suffer. It can also be used as the dark cloak for classroom control by a teacher. It can inhibit

FIGURE 3.1. THE QUESTION OF CONTENT COVERAGE

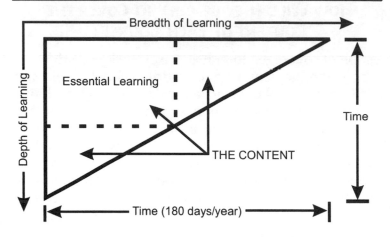

FIGURE 3.2. THE CONTENT COVERAGE PERSPECTIVE

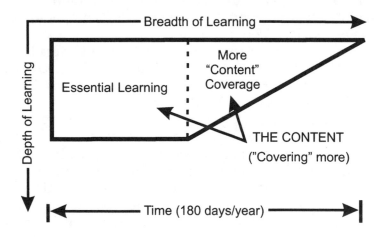

student initiation, discussion, and higher-order and creative thinking, and usually results in the one best method or the one correct answer. As a result, the need to cover the material may be the greatest roadblock to student comprehension at the high school level.

While there are those who argue that ELT will result in less material being covered (the breadth of the curriculum), one should consider the degree to which the material will be uncovered or learned (the depth of the curriculum) (see Figure 3.3). If we are concerned about student learning and the retention of learning, as we should be, then the latter has a greater impact than the former. In terms of learning and retention, the critical elements of the curriculum need to be the focus of classroom instruction and integrated across the curriculum. Essentially, the debate boils down to how all of the potential curriculum content is allocated during time that is available during the normal school year. There is a certain amount of "essential" content that students need to master in the adopted curriculum, regardless of whether the breadth or the depth of curriculum content is the focus.

FIGURE 3.3. THE DEPTH OF LEARNING PERSPECTIVE

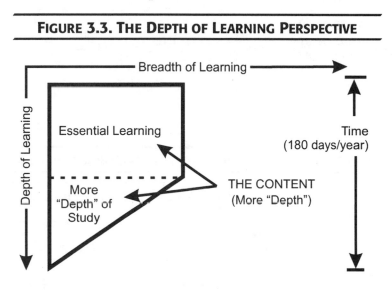

Finally, one factor that is lost in the debate over coverage versus content is that students will have the opportunity to select more courses and, with a 4x4 ELT model, a greater opportunity to accelerate the completion of the scope and sequence of courses in a particular discipline than with a traditional schedule. Figures 3.4 to 3.7 (pp. 88–89) outline a 4-year scope and sequence for a student at MHS. These figures are also referred to when we illustrate the additional adaptations that were made to meet the individual needs of students, to accommodate different curricular areas, and to accelerate the scope and sequence of courses in a variety of disciplines. For example, notice that it is conceivable for a student to begin with a two-year sequence in Algebra 1 as a freshman and still complete AP Calculus by the senior year, or to participate in the performing arts for four years as a

FIGURE 3.4. TYPICAL STUDENT SCHEDULE—FRESHMAN YEAR

Period Times		1997-98 Academic School Day Schedule			
		Fall Semester		Spring Semester	
		Day A	Day B	Day A	Day B
Period 1 7:50–9:13		Biology		English 1	
Period 2 9:23–10:46	Homeroom 9:16–9:20	World Studies 1		Algebra 1B	
Period 3 10:49–12:44	10:49–11:19 11:31–12:01 12:14–12:44	Band/ Chorus	P.E.	Band/ Chorus	Health & Reading
Period 4 12:47–2:10		Algebra 1A		Spanish 1	

FIGURE 3.5. TYPICAL STUDENT SCHEDULE—SOPHOMORE YEAR

Period Times		1997-98 Academic School Day Schedule			
		Fall Semester		Spring Semester	
		Day A	Day B	Day A	Day B
Period 1 7:50–9:13		English 2		Chemistry	
Period 2 9:23–10:46	Homeroom 9:16–9:20	Algebra 2		World Studies 2	
Period 3 10:49–12:44	10:49–11:19 11:31–12:01 12:14–12:44	Band/ Chorus	P.E.	Band/ Chorus	Health
Period 4 12:47–2:10		Spanish 2		Spanish 3	

FIGURE 3.6. TYPICAL STUDENT SCHEDULE—JUNIOR YEAR

Period Times		1997-98 Academic School Day Schedule			
		Fall Semester		Spring Semester	
		Day A	Day B	Day A	Day B
Period 1 7:50–9:13		English/ Language Arts		Pre-Calculus	
Period 2 9:23–10:46	Homeroom 9:16–9:20	Anatomy & Physiology		U.S. History 1	
Period 3 10:49–12:44	10:49–11:19 11:31–12:01 12:14–12:44	Band/ Chorus	P.E.	Band/ Chorus	Problem Solving 1
Period 4 12:47–2:10		Geometry		Spanish 4	

FIGURE 3.7. STUDENT SCHEDULE—SENIOR YEAR

Period Times		1997-98 Academic School Day Schedule			
		Fall Semester		Spring Semester	
		Day A	Day B	Day A	Day B
Period 1 7:50–9:13		AP English		AP English	AP Calculus
Period 2 9:23–10:46	Homeroom 9:16–9:20	AP Calculus		U.S. History 2	
Period 3 10:49–12:44	10:49–11:19 11:31–12:01 12:14–12:44	Band/ Chorus	P.E.	Band/ Chorus	Problem Solving 2
Period 4 12:47–2:10		Theatre Arts	Art History	Physics	

full-year subject. While these aspects of the 4x4 ELT model are discussed more fully in response to specific questions, consider the overall impact that the implementation of the ELT schedule will have on students at MHS:

- *Students will complete more core academic courses.* As a result of the increase in the graduation requirements, all students will be required to enroll in and successfully complete four-years of the traditional academic courses, which is an increase of 25–50 percent in these core curricular areas for most students.

- *Students will complete more nonmandated academic courses.* All students will be required to enroll in and successfully complete at least three years of world languages, two years of fine arts classes, and two years of practical arts. This represents an increase of 25–100 percent in these core and non-mandated academic courses for all students.

HOW WILL A TEACHER DECIDE WHAT CONTENT TO KEEP AND WHAT TO LEAVE OUT OF A COURSE?

Teachers make decisions regarding the curriculum on a daily basis. Look at the average textbook in any discipline. Do teachers cover all the material in the textbook during the course of a school year or even during a subsection of a course. The answer is a resounding "No!"

Dealing with the curriculum in an ELT schedule is really no different, in terms of decision making, than dealing with the curriculum in any organization pattern or schedule. There simply is not enough time to cover everything that teachers feel is important. For this reason, there are locally adopted curriculum guides, or statewide curriculum frameworks, or nationally developed curriculum standards for virtually all disciplines. Teachers must decide what the essential learnings are for each curricular area; how they will know when students attain the knowledge, feelings, and skills associated with the essential learnings; and how much time they have available for the teaching and learning process. In most instances, the essential learnings are identified in the locally adopted curriculum or the state mandated curriculum frameworks. Therefore, given these parameters, the process of eliminating the nonessential components of the course curriculum becomes somewhat easier.

Such a concept has the support of many educators who cite the results of the Third International Math and Science Study (TIMMS) as a prime reason for reflecting on the "Nostalgia Curriculum" (i.e., the same old, boring, teacher-centered curriculum that most parents experienced). Many critics have indicated that the math and science curriculum in the United States tends to be "a mile wide and an inch deep." It is time to construct a spiraled curriculum that continually builds on prior learning. The scope and sequence of such a curriculum, the teaching and learning strategies employed with such a curriculum, and the means of assessing student progress would be based on

- Thinking and communicating,
- Gaining and applying knowledge and skills, and
- Working together and contributing to a learning community.

Such a curriculum would be based on finding information when it is needed, deciding what information is good and relevant to a particular situation, and manipulating the information to solve a problem, to answer a question, or to develop something new. It would replace the static acquisition of inert knowledge.

IS IT TRUE THAT STUDENT RETENTION OF LEARNING IS LOST WHEN A STUDENT MISSES A SEMESTER OF A GIVEN SUBJECT?

The question of retention of learning is still one of the most frequently asked questions with regard to ELT schedules. It is even more important to address this issue with regard to a 4x4 ELT model than with an AB ELT model. The answer is drawn from what both researchers and practitioner experience have found relative to student learning and long-term retention. Retention is the ability to remember what has been learned and has always been a desired outcome of teaching. To date, both quantitative and qualitative field-based findings indicate students do retain what they learn. After all, schools and teachers really do make positive contributions to the intellectual, social, emotional, and psychomoter development of students. The supporting evidence is found in the empirical studies on retention of learning from the field of cognitive psychology and the evaluation studies conducted by Harvard University, National Training Labs, the U.S. Department of the Navy, the U.S. Department of Education, and schools nationwide that use the 4x4 academic school day plan.

The experience of schools with the 4x4 plan over the last several years indicates that long-term retention is not a real problem. Teachers have reported that they could discern very little difference between the retention of students who had just recently completed a prerequisite course and other students with greater time lapses between courses. In addition, teachers noted that there has always been a need for some review after the summer recess at the beginning of the school year. Nonetheless, the addition of a semester away from a course, when added to the summer recess, did not increase the need for review.

Several cognitive psychology studies are applicable to the question of retention of learning in a 4x4 schedule. The most significant loss of retention of learning occurs within the first few weeks after the end of a course. This occurs primarily in the loss of retention of factual knowledge. After this initial period, there is a leveling off in terms of retention loss. In one study, researchers compared the learning of students at the end of a course, 4 months later, and again after 11 months. They discovered that students retained 85 percent of what they had originally learned after 4 months and 80 percent of what they had originally learned after 11 months. If those findings were extrapolated, the expectation is that students would retain slightly less than 80 percent of their original learning if an entire year came between enrollment in two sequential courses. Therefore, one could argue that students do forget more over time, but the benefits appear to outweigh the liabilities.

It was once assumed that retention of learning was inherent in people with good memories; that is, certain people had "good" memories and others didn't. However, recent research has indicated that the way something is taught and how well it is taught has a great deal to do with how well it is retained and whether it can be recalled for use at a later time. Anything that is not well learned is rapidly forgotten. Therefore, anything worth teaching should be taught well or "uncovered" in terms of understanding, not just presented in a once-over-lightly manner or "covered." We also know that individuals learn at different rates and through different modalities. Attention has recently focused on Howard Gardner's work on multiple intelligences, which indicates what many people have observed in the past in terms of the teaching and learning process—one size does *not* fit all. By utilizing a variety of teaching strategies and addressing a variety of learning modalities, students experience learning from a number of different perspectives. This will increase the likelihood that whenever a learning opportunity appears similar to a past learning experience (regardless of the discipline), the past learning experience will have a higher probability of transfer to the present situation. Hence, the greater the probability that the student will be able to recall the previous learning and apply it to the new experience.

Another interesting finding relates to the retention rates for different kinds of knowledge (i.e., the retention of facts is significantly lower than for the recall of higher-order cognitive processes such as the recognition, comprehension, and mental skills that are required to apply knowledge and skills to new situations. Similarly, earlier cognitive learning studies support the finding that the recall and recognition of facts or knowledge decline more quickly than the retention of comprehension items and concepts. Ostensibly, these studies indicate that B. F. Skinner was on target when he stated that "education is what's left when all the facts are forgotten." Furthermore, the studies cited provide evidence that learning at higher cognitive levels—comprehension and application on Bloom's taxonomy—may be lost less rapidly than learning at the lowest level—knowledge. Therefore, it may be more critical for teachers to review basic knowledge-level information (i.e., specific terminology and facts) at the beginning of a new course than to worry about whether or not students have retained the basic concepts taught in previous sequentially related courses. Not surprisingly, studies suggest that knowledge-level learning occurs more rapidly than comprehension or application. Thus, the knowledge that is lost more quickly over time also can be regained more quickly with review. Conversely, and more significant to argument that "less is more" and learning theory, are the findings that higher-order learning results take longer periods of time to achieve mastery, but also result in greater long-term retention. These findings certainly support the use of the longer periods of teaching-and-learning time provided for in the 4x4 ELT schedule.

In summary, the empirical research and practitioner evaluation results support student learning and retention in the 4x4 ELT scheduling. While the ability of students to retain information may decrease because of a gap in course sequence, retention of concepts and skills only decreases slightly.

IS STUDENT ACHIEVEMENT AFFECTED BY ELT?

Researchers gathered the data presented in Figure 3.8 from 62 schools in 22 states (Arizona, California, Colorado, Illinois, Indiana, Kentucky, Louisiana, Massachusetts, Maryland, North Carolina, Nebraska, Oklahoma, Ohio, Pennsylvania, South Carolina, Tennessee, Texas, Utah, Washington, Wisconsin, West Virginia, and Wyoming). Not all of the schools responded with data for each of the factors listed in the figure. Also, because most of the states use the ACT examination as the primary test for college entrance, the number of schools responding to the SAT examination question (eight schools in this study) had a wider variance in scores than did the schools that use the ACT scores.

FIGURE 3.8. STUDENT ACHIEVEMENT AND ELT SCHEDULES (COSTA & TAYLOR, 1998)

Factor	Increase	Stable	Decrease	No Response
A Grades	43.3%	33.3%	10.0%	23.4%
B Grades	80.8%	3.8%	3.8%	11.6%
C Grades	5.0%	15.0%	70.0%	10.0%
D Grades	4.8%	9.5%	76.2%	9.5%
Failing Grades	20.0%	12.0%	56.0%	13.0%
AP Examinations	71.4%	14.3%	14.3%	0%
ACT Examinations	44.0%	40.0%	0%	16.0%
SAT Examinations	50.0%	0%	37.5%	12.5%
State Testing	69.0%	3.4%	24.1%	3.5%

It is important to note that student achievement, as indicated by class grades and norm-referenced test scores, did not always improve with ELT schedules. However, in most cases where grades and tests scores decreased, it was generally errors of omission prior to implementing the plan that created the potential for the lack of success. Two primary factors were the failure to identify clearly the reasons for implementing the change to an ELT schedule and the failure to gain the support of key stakeholders. In other instances, the necessary planning and preparation, including professional development activities for teachers, was poorly executed or lacking altogether prior to implementing the ELT schedule. In such instances, the implementation of any plan would face serious obstacles.

WHAT EFFECT WILL A 4x4 ELT MODEL HAVE ON STUDENTS WHO ARE APPLYING FOR ADMITTANCE TO COLLEGES AND UNIVERSITIES?

There are no reports of students not being accepted to the college or university of their choice because they were applying from a school with an

ELT schedule. In fact, because admission officers still focus on the student's program of studies in high school, the grades that they earn, their norm-referenced and criterion-referenced test scores, their cocurricular activities, and so forth, students who graduate from schools with an ELT schedule have an advantage over students who graduate from a traditional school with six or seven classes per day. As noted earlier, students in a school with an ELT schedule tend to achieve better grades in their classes, score better on standardized tests, and take more courses in the core curricular areas. They also have an opportunity to take more enrichment courses.

Students can take more courses in an ELT schedule and accelerate the scope and sequence of courses in a 4x4 ELT model. However, as Figures 3.4 to 3.7 (pp. 88–89) illustrate, attempts should be made to balance the classes for students in a semesterized schedule (i.e., English and math courses during one semester and history and science courses another semester, or a similar configuration). Also, attempts should be made to schedule English and math classes during the fall semester for seniors. In this way, students will have earned final grades in these courses when submitting their transcripts to colleges and universities.

WHAT DOES THE ELT CLASSROOM LOOK LIKE?

The ELT classroom is an excellent opportunity for teachers to establish any number of physical configurations of students' desks and chairs so that they become learning stations. The traditional rows of five and six students facing the teacher's desk or lectern soon become clusters of four and six where students are facing each other rather than looking at one another's backs. These learning stations provide an excellent opportunity for small group interaction among students, helping them fine-tune their communication and collaboration skills. At the same time, teachers have an opportunity to move about the classroom challenging each group to become innovative, independent learners. The ELT classroom becomes more student-centered, offering a variety of opportunities for students to take responsibility for their own learning. It also gives students a way to discover new and more efficient methods of learning and understanding. Teachers with more time to work with students during each ELT period are more inclined to allow students to be more active learners because there is less reliance on lecturing for the entire ELT period.

WHAT WILL A TEACHER BE ABLE TO ACCOMPLISH IN AN ELT PERIOD THAT THE TEACHER CANNOT ACCOMPLISH IN A TRADITIONAL 45- to 55-MINUTE PERIOD?

In the traditional 45- to 55-minute class period, the teacher is often rushed to introduce, to develop, and bring to closure the daily lesson. This occurs for a number of different reasons. First, most teachers, after getting their students settled, taking attendance, and reviewing the prior day's lesson have already spent a good portion of their class time. The introduction of new concepts and new content is generally done by way of directed instruction, leaving little opportunity for the students to dissect the lesson, construct their own meaning from the lesson, and interact with other students. More importantly the teacher's ability to test for understanding is inhibited during the initial and critical components of the lesson. The race against time and the class dismissal bell is often a source of frustration and anxiety for both students and teachers. Teachers often find themselves holding their students after the bell as they frantically attempt to bring the lesson to closure and explain the daily homework assignment.

In some disciplines, such as the practical arts, fine arts, and physical education, the traditional 45- to 55-minute period is not only less desirable for delivering instruction than a long block of time, but it may actually prevent substantial learning from occurring because of the time needed to prepare for the class and the time needed to put materials away and prepare for the next class. For example, consider the plight of physical education teachers. After students dress for class, after attendance is taken, and after teachers explain the daily activity, students generally have no more than 15–20 minutes to actually engage in the activity before returning to the locker room to change clothes for their next class. If the class activities are to take place outdoors, additional time is lost traveling from the locker room to the outdoor facility and back. A similar amount of instructional time is lost preparing for and closing the daily class in the practical arts and the fine arts. Although the down time at the beginning and end of these classes will still be experienced, it will not be experienced on a daily basis.

In the ELT period, teachers can drastically change their delivery of instruction because the daily amount of time is no longer a constraint. Teaching methods and instructional strategies that were not practical in the shorter periods are now useful and accessible. Teachers often discover through experimentation with multiple teaching models the different learning styles of their students, which helps them plan more effective lessons.

With the race against time a thing of the past, teachers can constantly test for understanding throughout the ELT period and thoroughly explain the night's homework assignments before the class is dismissed. Teachers also indicate that they can develop entire concepts in a single classroom period.

WILL TEACHERS BE ABLE TO KEEP STUDENTS INTERESTED FOR THE ENTIRE ELT PERIOD? DON'T FOUR 80- TO 90-MINUTE CLASSES MAKE FOR A LONG, BORING DAY FOR BOTH TEACHERS AND STUDENTS?

The ELT period challenges teachers to change how they plan their classes and how they keep students engaged. By adopting multiple teaching strategies and methodologies as well as providing students with the opportunity to be more active learners in the classroom, teachers are able to maintain student interest and involvement in the lesson for the entire class period.

Although there are fewer transitions in the school day between classes, there are a number of transitions within each class. We know that the average attention span for high school students on any given activity is anywhere from 20 to 50 minutes. Therefore, it is incumbent on teachers to vary the type and length of their teaching activities. The variety of activities, the pacing of the activities, and the transition from one activity to another help keep students engaged. Students have reported that they receive more individual attention, find it easier to concentrate on class work, have more time to complete work, better understand their homework assignments, and feel less stressed and rushed in an ELT classroom.

Teachers also feel that the day seems to fly by for them. However, teachers also state that they were exhausted by the end of the day during the initial year of an ELT schedule. This is easy to understand because in a briskly paced ELT class a teacher engages in a number of different activities using multiple teaching strategies. For example, after reviewing the prior day's lesson using the question-and-answer method, the teacher may introduce new information and break the class into groups to do a cooperative learning activity. At the conclusion of the activity the groups share their findings with each other, which leads to a general class discussion. The teacher then tests for understanding by assigning individual seat-work followed by another question-and-answer period before bringing the lesson to closure with yet another activity or assignment. Homework is then assigned and the students are given sample problems or asked to answer sample questions to make sure that they understand their assignment. This example illustrates how the ELT classroom can provide both the teacher and the student with a number of different opportunities to engage in the lesson. Because both teachers and students are actively engaged in what is going on in the classroom, the time seems to pass quickly for everyone.

WHAT PREVENTS A TEACHER FROM USING PART OF THE ELT PERIOD TO ALLOW STUDENTS TO VIEW FILMS OR DO HOMEWORK?

With the concern that teachers generally express regarding covering the content of a course, there should be little time available for teachers to spend viewing films or allowing students to do their homework. More direct supervision of those teachers who do not feel comfortable using a variety of instructional strategies or who have not developed a sufficient repertoire of strategies to "fill" the available class time with such activities helps ensure that this is not a problem.

On the other hand, all written work in a classroom is not homework. By definition, homework is a learning activity that is completed at home or at least outside of normal class time. The written assignments students frequently complete in class are generally guided or independent practice, which teachers use to assess the learning needs of students or to test for understanding. Using class work as a means of assessing student progress allows teachers to individualize their attention and provide tutorials for students. These strategies are frequently cited as two of the major advantages of the ELT schedule.

Generally, this issue is a nonissue for most faculty members and should be dealt with just as any other isolated instruction problem is dealt with in the school. When both teachers and students are jointly responsible for actively engaging in the teaching and learning process with a rich and ambitious curriculum, it is unlikely that students will be doing homework in the classroom.

WILL A 4x4 ELT MODEL ADVERSELY AFFECT PERFORMING ARTS PROGRAMS?

The performing arts programs that are included as part of the normal daily schedule can be adversely impacted by a 4x4 ELT model. Components of these programs, such as band, symphony, and choral groups, generally function as full-year programs. Therefore, accommodations need to be made to allow students in the performing arts to continue to develop their skills and talents throughout the entire school year. Such accommodations can be made in a variety of forms (e.g., establishing one shorter period for the entire school year, scheduling classes on alternate days, or a format unique to a particular school). To illustrate this point, the question of the impact of a semester ELT plan was raised early in the planning phase at MHS. A commitment was given to music teachers, students, and parents that the integrity of the music program would not suffer and every effort would be made to improve the music program at MHS. From this frame of reference, the members of the music department, in conjunction with the administration, established a format that allowed students to participate in both the band and choral programs. As Figures 3.4 to 3.7 (pp. 88–89) indicate, students could elect the performing arts during each of their high school years.

First, the instrumental and choral teachers in the Milford School Department are itinerants (i.e., they teach a portion of the school day in different schools). As a result, one ELT period per day did not rotate like the remaining three periods. Second, the band and choral programs were scheduled on alternate days for the entire school year. Third, a practice schedule was established that would allow students to participate in the band and choral programs concurrently. Students elected the "Vocal, Instrumental, and Performance (VIP)" program. Within this framework, some students were able to concentrate on just instrumental music or just the choral music, while others split their time between the instrumental music and the choral music programs. Figure 3.9 illustrates the practice schedule that was established for students enrolled in the performing arts.

The key point in this example is not the schedule, but the cooperation between the administration and the members of the music department to resolve a potential problem and establish procedures that benefited students. Since the inception of the VIP program at MHS, the enrollment in the music program has risen dramatically (the combined membership in the chorus and band has risen from 160 students to 240 students).

WILL THE 4x4 ELT MODEL ADVERSELY AFFECT PHYSICAL EDUCATION PROGRAMS?

One of the immediate gains for a physical education program in an ELT schedule is the increase in class time for a variety of activities. No longer will 50 percent or more of the class time be utilized in the locker room and in organizing preparation for activities. However, one of the concerns of the physical education teachers is the impact a 4x4 ELT model has on the scope and sequence of curricular offerings in a semester program. Figure 3.10 (pp. 101–103) is an example of a diversified program that was developed to

(Text continues on page 103.)

FIGURE 3.9. MHS PERFORMING ARTS PRACTICE SCHEDULE

Practice Schedule	Performing Arts Practice Times by Dan Evans, Director of Music
Day 1	11:20–12:00 • Full Chorus meets • Band and Strings meet without Chorus members 12:05–12:45 • Full Band and Strings meet • Chorus meets without Band and String members
Day 2	11:20–12:00 • Full Band and Strings meet • Chorus meets without Band and String members 12:05–12:45 • Full Chorus meets • Band and Strings meet without Chorus members
Day 3	11:20–12:00 • Full Band and Strings meet • Chorus meets without Band and String members 12:05–12:45 • Full Chorus meets • Band and Strings meet without Chorus members
Day 4	11:20–12:00 • Full Orchestra meets • Band and Chorus meet without Orchestra members 12:05–12:45 • Full Band or Chorus meets (varied)
Day 5	11:20–12:00 • Full Band or Chorus meets (varied) 12:05–12:45 • Recital period for all VIP members

FIGURE 3.10. PHYSICAL EDUCATION AND HEALTH

Comprehensive Physical Education, Health and Wellness Syllabus
by John Dagnese, Peter Filosa, and Nicholas Zacchilli

◆ Introduction to the program
  • Class #1: Distribute and discuss the syllabus, activities to be offered, length of units, goals and objectives, instructor's expectations of students, and methods of evaluation.

◆ Unit 1: Introduction to Wellness and Weight Training
  • Class #2: Anatomy (i.e., muscle groups, skeletal system, stretching and exercises, and the relationship of each to particular activities) and use of equipment (i.e., care and safety, spotting procedures, demonstration of exercise, and determining a student's maximum effort);
  • Class #3: Weight room (i.e. using record sheets and 70% of maximum effort, assignment to groups based upon maximum effort, and review of spotting instruction on free weights);
  • Class #4: Opening activities and stretching, introduction to cardiovascular activities, flexibility testing, and vertical jump testing; and,
  • Class #5: Opening activities and stretching, re-test for maximum effort, written evaluation and introduction to walking.

◆ Unit 2: Walking
  • Class #6: Instruction on monitoring heart rate, stretching techniques, mile walk pre-test, and postexercise heart rate;
  • Class #7: Record resting heart rate, stretching, one 1.5 mile walk, rest and fitness handout review, 1 mile slow walk, and postexercise heart rate and cooling down stretching;
  • Class #8: Record resting heart rate, stretching, 2.5 mile walk, postexercise heart rate and cool down, and review of evaluation test requirements; and,
  • Class #9: Evaluation test, 2.0 mile walk in 30 minutes, written test, and introduction to Unit 3.

◆ Unit 3: Badminton
  • Class #10: Introduction to basic badminton skills, rules, and strategies; practice doubles games; and team and tournament setup;
  • Class #11: Tournament play (round robin) and record results;
  • Class #12: Tournament play continued;
  • Class #13: Tournament play continued and playoffs and championship matches;
  • Class #14: Individual skill evaluation, written test, and introduction to Unit 4.

(Figure continues on next page.)

- Unit 4: Cardiopulmonary Resuscitation (CPR) and First Aid
  - Class #15: Introduction to CPR (video), liabilities and other issues, and assessment of victim;
  - Class #16: Choking (video), group practice (checking airways and Heimlich Maneuver), nonbreathing situations (video), and group practice;
  - Class #17: Unconscious victims (video), group practice relative to the evaluation of the victim, heart disease and CPR (videos), and begin group practices of CPR skills;
  - Class #18: Complete group practice of CPR skills, introduce First Aid and related skills (bleeding, shock, fractures, sudden illness, and so forth); and,
  - Class #19: Complete First Aid review, written test on CPR and First Aid, and introduction to Unit 5.

- Unit 5: Selectives (Tennis and Softball)
  - Class #20: Tennis—teach and review rules and strategies; the serve, forehand, and backhand; and establish double pairings for tournament play *or* softball—review basic team play, explain safety procedures and divide class for tournament play;
  - Class #21: Tennis—team pairings begin round robin doubles tournament *or* softball—assigned teams begin class series;
  - Class #22: Tennis and softball tournament and series play continues;
  - Class #23: Tennis and softball tournament and series play continues; and,
  - Class #24: Written tests and introduction to Unit 6.

- Unit 6: Aerobics
  - Class #25: Explain and select cardiovascular aerobic activities (i.e., water aerobics, lap swim, low impact video or jogging);
  - Class #26: Review heart rate material for all activities; calculate resting, maximum and target heart rates; and endurance pretest and record results;
  - Class #27: Stretching, water aerobics (increase activity time); lap swim (increase distances); aerobics (incorporate step boards); and postactivity stretching and cool down;
  - Class #28: Continue all aerobic activities and increase time and distances; and,
  - Class #29: Aerobic activities skill tests, written tests, and introduction to Unit 7.

- Unit 7: Golf
  - Class #30: Golf techniques for the short game (video) and skills practice (i.e., grip, stance, and strokes);
  - Class #31: Use of 9 iron and putter; and pitch and putt practice on minicourse;
  - Class #32: Tournament play (scorecards) and record scores of foursomes;
  - Class #33: Play new course layout, record scores, and handout study guides; and,
  - Class #34: Written test and introduction to Unit 8.

♦ Unit 8: Nutrition
- Class #35: Discuss the importance of good nutrition, nutritional values of foods, the basic food groups and essential nutrients, and evaluate personal eating habits;
- Class #36: Discuss sources of energy from foods, energy requirements for various people and activities, and body compositions;
- Class #37: Discuss nutrition and its relationship to life expectancy; weight maintenance, weight loss, and weight gain; and caloric relationship to healthy nutrition and diet-related diseases;
- Class #38: Discuss sports and nutrition, personal diets and eating habits of students, and myths and misconceptions about eating as they relate to athletic performance; and,
- Class #39: Written test and introduction to Unit 9.

♦ Unit 9: Selectives (Volleyball, Water Safety, and Recreational Swimming)
- Class #40: Volleyball—teach and review skills (i.e., passing, setting, and hitting) or Water safety—self-rescues (i.e., treading water and survival float);
- Class #41: Volleyball—review rules and strategies or water safety—rescues (i.e., water entries, side carry, torpedo buoys);
- Class #42: Volleyball—establish team pairings and begin tournament play or water safety—review rescues using ring buoy and reach pole;
- Class #43: Volleyball—continue tournament play or water safety—skill test and recreational swimming;
- Class #44: Volleyball—tournament championships and written test or water safety—written test and recreational swimming; and,
- Class #45: Complete semester activities, clear lockers, collect locks, review final grades, and so forth.

---

address the concerns of physical education teachers. In this model, classes meet on alternate days for one semester for an ELT period.The semester syllabus outlined in Figure 3.10, provides students with a comprehensive physical education and health program involving individual and team activities that focus on competitive and life-long activities, nutrition, and wellness. It also stresses the development of cognitive, affective, and psychomotor knowledge and skills, and reinforces the learning that students attain in other disciplines. In this manner, the 4x4 ELT model helps integrate the various disciplines.

WILL THE 4x4 ELT MODEL MEET THE
NEEDS OF SPECIAL NEEDS STUDENTS?

The ELT schedule is an asset to teaching students with learning difficulties in both a regular classroom and in a resource room setting. Most students with learning disabilities or difficulties require a multisensory approach to learn new concepts effectively. The ELT periods gives teachers the time to use a variety of teaching methods and strategies to actively engage special needs students in the learning process. Many of these students learn best when directly involved in an activity. The ELT classroom builds in respectable "chunks" of time in which students can complete tasks, activities, and assignments with a more thorough understanding of the concepts being taught.

The traditional six- or seven-period day required special needs students to make six or seven transitions per day, to adapt to different sets of teacher expectations, and to deal with a fragmented curriculum. In an ELT classroom, teachers can establish routines and standards at the start of each course and for each ELT period. First, by establishing routines quickly and efficiently, the teacher's expectations become clear and students know the rules associated with being a successful learner in the classroom. Once the rules are established and consistently practiced, teachers can focus on the academic subject matter and students can participate more readily in the activities at hand. Second, with expectations and routines clearly established, the academic goals, objectives, and activities become the focus at the onset of each ELT period.

A variety of instructional strategies and learning activities have replaced the "drill and kill" activities often associated with the development of basic skills for special needs students. Actively involving special needs students with individual and group projects helps to keep them on task. The 4x4 ELT model allows special needs students to function within established norms and routines, while experiencing the same variety of classes along with focused activities that improve student learning and retention.

WILL THE 4x4 ELT MODEL MEET
THE NEEDS OF ESL STUDENTS?

Just as the ELT classroom can serve as a basis for improving learning for special needs students, ESL students can also benefit from the diversity and variety of learning opportunities an ELT schedule can provide. The thematic activity web can be used as a template for a class, a unit of study, or for projecting a total course of studies. Because of the diversity of students in the typical ESL classroom, the thematic activity web can be used to organize a variety of learning activities that can concurrently be implemented for individual students or groups of students without losing sight of the major theme—literacy.

With literacy as the theme, the ESL classroom can focus on reading, writing, and oral communications using a series of the strategies outlined in Figure 3.11 in a single ELT period.

As Figure 3.11 illustrates, the theme is the key for planning lessons for an ESL classroom. The ELT classroom provides teachers with the time to develop a variety of activities to support the central theme. These activities do not stand alone as teaching strategies, but rather ensure that the defined learning theme is the focus of classroom learning. The 4x4 ELT model affords ESL students a form of immersion that traditional schedules might preclude, along with a variety of offerings and experiences with different students.

HOW DOES A 4x4 ELT MODEL DEAL WITH AP COURSES?

A primary dilemma with the 4x4 ELT model is the scheduling of AP classes. If the classes are scheduled during the fall semester, students generally complete the course or courses by January of the school year. For seniors this is ideal because the grades will appear on their transcripts. However, the AP examinations are not administered until May of the spring semester. Once again, the retention of factual information is a problem. If the courses are offered during the spring semester, the examinations are administered prior to the completion of the course. Again, this poses a problem.

A variety of approaches have been adopted to address the issue of AP classes and AP examinations. Some schools offer AP classes as full-year courses during ELT periods. This almost doubles the amount of time that students spend studying the subject matter in a particular course. The downside of this approach is the careful planning that is required during the underclass years to meet the graduation requirements in other disciplines while ensuring that they also meet the prerequisites for the AP course.

Another approach is to offer a tutorial to students prior to the administration of the AP examinations. This provides students with a review of the subject matter prior to the examination. A middle of the road approach is illustrated in Figure 3.7 (p. 89). In this instance the AP course meets every day for an ELT period during the fall semester and on alternate days for an ELT

FIGURE 3.11. THE THEMATIC ACTIVITY WEB

Frames of Reference for an ESL Classroom
by Sal Ferreira

♦ Interactive conversation is constant (i.e., student to student; student to teacher; within groups, pairs, and cross-level support), using the mechanics of transfer from the primary language;

♦ Experiential activities or the use of learned classroom vocabulary and grammar are applied to real school situations (i.e., through the use of learned communication skills, students begin to handle their own school problems without a translator or school personnel);

♦ Grammar-focused activities utilize exercises with jumping off points for usage in writing and conversation (i.e., a simple question can provide the framework for vocabulary, grammar teaching through the process of a meaningful conversation);

♦ A variety of learning stations or areas provide students with an opportunity to experience a total physical response (i.e., students can move freely, depending on the lesson, to areas of the classroom for different individual and group learning activities, and may use available audio and computer technology);

♦ Genuine problem-solving activities are provided for the ESL students that require them to generate ideas and materials for group discussions (i.e., by working toward solutions to problems, the theme of literacy is constantly reinforced);

♦ Listening activities such as dictation and audiotapes are used with the teacher as the coach to clarify pronunciation and assist in the expansion of vocabulary as the discussion progresses;

♦ A variety of reading activities are used—both aloud and silent reading—to develop comprehension through discussions and written exercises;

♦ All activities involve some type of writing exercises to assist students to organize their ideas in their primary language and in first language transfer; and,

♦ A variety of games and puzzles (i.e., word games, crossword puzzles, computer grammar and vocabulary games) are all used to reinforce learning.

period during the spring semester. In this adaptation, students spend more class hours studying the subject matter than in either a traditional schedule or a single semester in an ELT schedule. They also experience the course activities up to the time of the AP examination.

The downside of this approach is the need to offer a variety of classes that also meet on an alternate-day schedule. However, establishing a variety of enrichment classes that meet on alternate days for one semester can provide "bridges" in subject matter for individuals concerned with retention of learning. The approach that is ultimately chosen needs to address the specific concerns of your school. Again, one size does not fit all and a single model should not be adopted to solve a similar problem at different schools.

Do District and School Policies Need to be Changed to Accommodate an ELT Schedule?

There are few policies that a school district needs to consider changing when moving to an ELT schedule. Perhaps, the most significant change involves altering graduation requirements because students will be enrolling in more courses and accumulating many more course credits throughout their four years of high school. For example, if a 4x4 ELT model replaces a traditional 7-period day schedule, students who normally took 5–6 courses per year with study halls for each of their 4 years would complete 20–25 courses by graduation. A graduating senior completing 4 years of 4x4 ELT schedule with no study halls will complete 32 courses. Because students will take more courses in the core curricular areas, it is also likely that a school district would want to consider increasing the requirements for graduation in specific curricular areas.

What Impact will the ELT Schedule have on Teacher and Student Attendance?

Both student and teacher daily attendance tends to improve in schools that have adopted an schedule. As Figure 3.12 indicates, the improvement in student attendance was one of the more consistent factors indicating a positive impact of changing to an ELT schedule. Similarly, the daily attendance of teachers also tended to improve. Currently, there is only speculation regarding the reasons for the improvement in attendance of both students and teachers in an ELT schedule. Student indications range from "I like this schedule better" or "the day goes by a lot quicker with a lot less stress," to the feeling that they "cannot afford to miss that much class time because they will have too much work to make up." A number of teachers have indicated similar feelings from similar perspectives. However, more studyis needed to establish the relationship between improved student and teacher attendance and the ELT schedule.

FIGURE 3.12. STUDENT ATTENDANCE WITH ELT SCHEDULES (COSTA & TAYLOR, 1998)

Factor	Increase	Stable	Decrease	No Response
Attendance	43.3%	33.3%	10.0%	13.4%

WHAT IMPACT WILL TEACHER OR STUDENT ABSENCES HAVE ON THE TEACHING AND LEARNING PROCESS IN AN ELT SCHEDULE?

Most schools having success with ELT schedules claim that teacher-student relationships improve and that students invariably become more independent thinkers and learners. Improved student-teacher relationships bring about a better understanding of what is expected of the student when the teacher is absent and what responsibilities the student has for missed class time when they can't attend school.

If the ELT-schedule school commits to insuring that the curriculum continues in a teacher's absence, then the teaching and learning process will not be adversely affected. However, this requires individual teachers to be better organized when planning lessons for substitute teachers. Student dispositions toward substitute teachers also need to change. When teachers develop lessons that can be implemented by substitute teachers, they are more apt to hold their respective students accountable for completing the lessons whether they are present or not. Hence, teachers will need to be more responsible for developing lessons that are used in their absence, will need to make those lesson challenging and engaging enough to keep students on task, and will need to hold students accountable when the they return to the class.

On the other hand, when students are absent from school, they will shoulder a greater responsibility for makeup work. In the process of teaching students to become independent thinkers and learners, teachers need to make students more responsible for their own learning. It is true that there are fewer class meetings in the ELT-schedule courses and that there is a greater impact on students who miss classes. Nonetheless, as part of the process of preparing them for higher education and future careers, the students must develop both the responsibility and the accountability for the time that is missed from class.

WHAT IMPACT WILL THE ELT SCHEDULE HAVE ON STUDENT DISCIPLINE?

There are a number of reasons why schools that have adopted ELT schedules report fewer discipline problems. First, there are fewer times when students are passing between classes, which significantly reduces the number of opportunities students have to engage in confrontational situations with other students.

Second, the number of students disciplined for class cuts diminishes as students are held accountable to stricter attendance standards in the ELT-schedule school. Students realize that cutting a long-block class has a greater impact on their success in that class than was the case when class meetings were the traditional 45–55 minutes.

Third, there is more time on learning, fewer instances of nondirected instructional time such as study halls, and less downtime in most classes. Within the classroom setting, the establishment of a better understanding between students and teachers generally results in a more positive classroom environment. In schools that adopt a 4x4 ELT model, both teachers and students are able to start fresh at least twice per year.

Finally, it is well-known among educators that the best deterrent to discipline problems is a good lesson plan. Teachers moving to ELT classes are forced to rethink how they teach and how students learn, which often motivates them to be more innovative in planning lessons that keep students engaged for the entire class period. Students who are kept on task are less apt to engage in the kind of behaviors that bring about problems for their teachers and peers.

The data presented in Figure 3.13 (which draws on the same 62-school 22-state research discussed earlier regarding Figure 3.8, p. 94), supports the claim that the number of disciplinary problems tends to decrease when schools adopt an ELT schedule. Furthermore, the dropout rate, which tends to be associated with poor academic achievement, poor attendance, and disciplinary problems also tends to decrease in schools that adopt an ELT schedule.

**FIGURE 3.13. STUDENT SUSPENSIONS AND DROPOUTS
WITH ELT SCHEDULES (COSTA & TAYLOR, 1998)**

Factor	Increase	Stable	Decrease	No Response
Suspensions	26.3%	10.5%	56.0%	13.0%
Dropouts	9.5%	4.8%	76.2%	9.5%

HOW DO YOU DEAL WITH A TEACHER WHO REFUSES TO CHANGE INSTRUCTIONAL METHODS AND CONTINUES TO LECTURE FOR THE ENTIRE ELT PERIOD?

Teachers attempting to lecture for the entire ELT period generally discover that it is physically difficult to deliver three ELT lectures per day, and this becomes the most significant safeguard against its occurrence. Nonetheless, old habits die hard. For any number of reasons there will be a few teachers who will continue to lecture for a majority of the class period simply because they believe that lecture is the best method of instruction or because they have not developed additional instructional strategies. Ironically, teachers who refuse to change their methods to accommodate the student-centered classroom invariably bring unwanted attention to themselves, which attention becomes the very reason why they eventually turn to new methods.

Initially, school administrators are made aware of teachers who overly rely on the lecture method from direct observations or from the feedback they receive from students and parents. When they receive such information, it is crucial that they speak with the individual teachers to clarify expectations and to determine why there have been no changes in the delivery of instruction to accommodate student needs in the ELT schedule. Teachers need to understand that ELT periods require methods directed toward student-centered classrooms rather than lecture-based, teacher-centered classrooms.

Because most schools moving to an ELT schedule provide teachers with professional development opportunities to explore new teaching methodologies suitable for ELT classes, it is also reasonable to expect teachers to make use of the new strategies. On the other hand, it is also important to remember that teachers need time to adjust their methods as they try new approaches to delivering instruction, especially when they are being asked to rethink the way that they have been teaching throughout their tenure. As the initial year of implementation progresses and as more and more teachers share classroom successes with their colleagues, this becomes less and less of a problem.

WILL THE ELT SCHEDULE AFFECT EXTRACURRICULAR ACTIVITIES?

Insufficient meeting time and conflicts with meeting times have always been an issue for extracurricular organizations and their advisors, and it is still an issue in schools using ELT schedules. However, ELT schedules have not made the situation any worse, and with some creative planning, they can improve the situation. Building in "activity" periods is something that can be more readily accommodated in an ELT schedule than in a traditional six- or seven-period day.

It is important to understand that extracurricular activities have suffered in numbers and have fought for survival ever since students began working after school and making automobiles and insurance higher priorities than extracurricular activities. Time on learning is again a major culprit, as activity periods have been eliminated from school schedules so students can spend more time in academic classes.

Schools with ELT schedules still have the option of including an activity or "X" period for extracurricular organizations to meet daily, weekly, biweekly, or some other time frame. There are any number of possibilities for building activity time into the ELT schedule. It is the responsibility of each school to assess its needs and adjust the schedule accordingly.

SUMMARY

The road to success is almost always filled with bumps, potholes, and obstacles that constantly need repair. School personnel need to consider that excellence is a state of becoming rather than a state of being. Looking at our world, it is easy to see that change is inevitable, but it is more difficult to recognize that growth is optional. As a result, the apathy of many of the key stakeholders in our schools, who are happy with their little niche in the status quo, is a major obstacle to achieving excellence and equity for all students. However, by listening to the questions posed by key stakeholders and making adjustments for the uniqueness of a particular school, anticipating and preparing to respond to questions with both quantitative and qualitative data is a powerful tool for responding to those who resist change. An ELT schedule can be the vehicle for transforming schools of the twentieth century into the learning communities of the twenty-first century.

4

PLANNING FOR SUCCESS: INNOVATION AND SAMPLE LESSONS

In teaching, it is the method and not the content that is the message…the drawing out, not the pumping in.

Ashley Montagu

Planning lessons for ELT classes is no different than planning lessons for the traditional 45 to 55-minute class. In fact, planning lessons for ELT classes gives teachers the opportunity to develop their favorite teaching strategies and activities more fully, while introducing and using new strategies and activities. On the other hand, teachers cannot expect to rely solely on a single instructional strategy or activity in an ELT classroom.

The primary difference in the planning and preparation for the ELT class is that the teacher will have to develop lessons that are student-centered rather than teacher-centered. For many teachers, the need to be in control of the classroom at all times is a fundamental axiom of teaching at the high school level. As a result, teachers are not comfortable turning over a portion of the responsibility for learning to their students, even though that is how the student processes a situation or an activity that directly relates to student learning and retention. Unfortunately, the teacher-centered classroom and the student-centered classroom are opposite points of view. Additionally, many, if not most, high school teachers are being asked to change their perspectives and develop new instructional strategies late in their careers.

The dilemma of the old versus the new need not present an insurmountable obstacle to the ELT classroom. Teachers should not feel that they are being asked to abandon the instructional strategies and methods with which they are comfortable; rather, they need to expand their repertoire. They need to be cautious of overusing the expository and lecture methodology, and they need to give students more learning opportunities.

Teachers can be innovative in their planning because they now have more time to work with. The greatest challenge the instructor will face is the "pacing" of activities in the ELT class. It will take time for teachers to develop a rhythm and to discoverer which combinations of instructional strategies and activities are most suitable for their classes. It is also imperative that administrators and colleagues be supportive and patient with teachers who are attempting to develop and implement new ideas, new strategies, and new teaching procedures.

There is no right or wrong structure or formula for developing lesson plans for ELT periods. In fact there are a number of different templates a teacher may choose to use. Generally, in the planning of any lesson, long or short, identifying the lesson objectives is critical. It is also helpful to identify the teaching methods and activities that will be employed, the materials needed, the procedures, and the amount of to be time spent on each lesson activity.

Another critical aspect of the lesson planning process, is to provide teachers with opportunities to collaborate and share. Not only does collaboration improve camaraderie among colleagues, but many new methods and activities for the classroom can be explored. If the statement is made that "you can't teach an old dog new tricks," reflect upon the types of lessons, the variety of instructional strategies, and the risks that the veteran faculty at one high school was able to develop and implement. The remainder of this chapter is devoted to the lesson plans used by members of the MHS faculty during the 1997-98 school year.

Figure 4.1 is an example of how one veteran teacher approached the ELT classroom. Recognizing that ELT provided teachers with an opportunity to develop multidimensional lessons, planning proceeded from a variety of perspectives designed to engage students in a variety of activities, and their learning was assessed in ways that accommodated a number of learning styles. Thus, the teacher continually planned lessons from a several frames of reference and with a variety of activities in mind to stimulate student learning. Although all teachers begin with these thoughts in mind, the ELT schedule provides teachers with the opportunity to implement a variety of activities within a given period on a given day. Figure 4.1 lists the frames of reference that served as a guide in planning lessons for history and social science classes, although much of the same thinking is readily adaptable to other disciplines.

Beginning with the recognition that "one size does not fit all" allows teachers to formulate multiple strategies for the basic lesson plan to achieve a particular objective or objectives (see Figure 4.2, p. 117). Thereafter, noting and cataloging successes will provide colleagues with references that can be replicated and modified to meet the needs of different students within a particular class.

What follows Figures 4.1 and 4.2 are sample teaching lessons that were developed through the collaborative efforts of the Milford High School teaching staff. While our teachers continue to develop lessons for ELT periods, they, like their colleagues around the country continue to seek new and efficient ways to develop interesting and well paced lessons that are student centered for ELT classes.

FIGURE 4.1. PLANNING FOR THE CLASSROOM

Frames of Reference
by Joseph Brucato
History and Social Science Department Chair

♦ Students learn less through the traditional lecture format where they are passive receptors of information than if they are active participants in a learning experience. They learn more when provided with an opportunity to express their own ideas, to be creative, and to use their powers of imagination to uncover and discover the meaning of a curricular objective.

♦ Students work better when their self-esteem is boosted. When teachers understand an individual's talent, the teachers can allow students to shape their individual skills around the curriculum objective.

♦ Students who have developed good writing skills or who are developing such skills can be provided with the opportunity to express themselves in journals, diary entries, skits, play writing, dialogues, and editorials.

♦ Students who have an interest and talent in the visual arts can be given an opportunity to express their ideas graphically, visually, artistically, and through illustrations.

♦ Students who are musicians or vocalists can utilize those talents to connect to a period in history by performing a composition from that era or writing their own music or lyrics.

♦ Student leaders in the class can function as organizers within the groups. They can apply their skills in student government or their experiences as designated leaders or captains in cocurricular activities to keep everyone focused.

♦ Students interested in theatre can apply their creative talents as actors, directors, or choreographers to role-playing and simulating scenes from a particular event or situation.

♦ Students who appear to be stubborn or cynical can be provided an opportunity to apply their revisionist attitudes to lash out at the accepted norms of historical study. They can be provided a productive forum to lampoon, parody, and satirize politicians, events, and society.

♦ Students who tend to be more vocal in class can be provided an opportunity to use their talents and characteristics to lead debates.

♦ Students who may want a career as an engineer or an architect can use their talents, skills, and interests to create original blueprints, designs, temples, pyramids, and skyscrapers.

♦ Look for the knowledge and skills that students bring to the classroom setting, and develop activities that will allow students to use such assets to develop new knowledge and skills, and to teach others the essential learnings of the curriculum.

FIGURE 4.2. FRAMEWORKS FOR A LESSON PLAN

Frameworks for a Lesson Plan
by Joseph Brucato
History and Social Science Department Chair

Sample Lesson #1—Improving on a Theme

1. The teacher spends 10–15 minutes introducing a topic to the class. He then divides class into groups of fours (or fives).
2. The instructor now hands out a direction sheet to each group. There are four to five different activities on the same topic: (See attached sheet)
   - Write a diary entry or journal about a famous person in that time period
   - Draw a satirical cartoon which pokes fun at/or lampoons a particular event or person
   - Write a dialogue between two historical personalities with contrasting points of view
   - Look up 10 terms from a given section of the text and write a synopsis of that section using those terms
3. Each student in his respective group selects an activity.
4. Each student has approximately 30–40 minutes to complete the activity.
5. Once the exercise is completed, the students in each group have 5 minutes to explain what they have done.
6. A group spokesperson will then summarize the activities of his associates for the rest of the class. (5 minutes per group)
7. The other groups in the class compare and contrast what they have accomplished utilizing those same exercises.
8. The teacher summarizes the activity.

Sample Lesson #2—Portfolio of Historical Creativity

1. The teacher spends 10–15 minutes presenting a general overview of the historical topic.
2. Students are divided into groups according to reference. There are four groups:
   - Drawing/Painting/Illustrating Group
   - Writers/Satirists/Journalists Group
   - Hands-on Activities Group
   - Cartographers Group

(Figure continues on next page.)

3. All groups are given the same theme to research. Each category represents a different view of that same theme. Thus, the drawers will produce a comic book, design a building, or create a watercolor depiction of some event or person. The writers will design a short skit, develop a newspaper, or write a satirical essay. The hands-on group will create some type of display, such as a battle scene, a rendition of an historical invention, or a board game. Finally, the cartographers group will create a map lesson based upon the geography or demographics of the time period. (50–60 minutes)

Sample Lesson #3—Music in the Classroom

1. The teacher assigns a theme and divides the class into three groups.
2. One group will be the lyricists, a second will be the producers, and the third will be the musicians.
3. The lyricists will write the words to a song that lampoons, parodies, satirizes, or reflects events within the given theme. The musician's group will discuss various sounds that they can use as a background to the lyrics. *Important*—Although there is likely to be a musician or two in the class, their presence is not necessary. Students can record a cassette of sampled sounds (hammer sounds, machines, drills, explosions, drum beats, etc.) to represent the angst, violence, or the ups and downs of a given event. A rap song, ballad, or a student dictating the lyrics to a prerecorded background of sounds or music will do. Finally, the producers will work in conjunction with both groups to coordinate the entire product. They will make the decisions as to what lyric or sound is appropriate.
4. The project should take from one to two 83-minute periods.

ENGLISH LANGUAGE ARTS

Teacher: Jim McCallum

Topic: Breaking Women Stereotyping Through Literature

Course/Subject: AP Literature and Composition

Time to Complete: 3 ELT periods

Teaching Methods: Cooperative group learning, Q&A, guided practice

Materials: Excerpts from John Gray's *Men Are From Mars, Women Are From Venus* (see attached).

Objectives: Students will demonstrate an understand of the 19th century perception of women in preparation for reading *The Awakening* and *A Doll's House.*

Procedure: *Minutes:*

Day 1: *No introduction to the unit!* (This is very important.) Pass out "snippets" handout and have class read it. The reaction should be quite interesting (approx. 15–20 mins.). Divide them into two groups—male and female. The rest of the period they will formulate some ideas for a panel discussion based on Gray's work.   85–90

Day 2: The entire block will be used to prepare for their panel discussion, which will take place on the following day. Parameters for the panel: 85–90

- Each person from each panel will make a 1-minute statement.
- After the statement there will be a 1-minute response from the other panel (open to anyone).
- After all statements/responses are concluded, there will be an open discussion about how men and their relationships with women (and vice versa) are stereotyped.

Day 3: First 60 minutes will be the panel discussion. The teacher will serve as moderator and timekeeper. The remaining class time will be used to draw conclusions based on the discussion. This serves as an excellent segue into *The Awakening* and *A Doll's House,* two works that emphasize strong female characters.   85–90

Notes:

- ♦ Students comment that the panels and subsequent discussions really helped in changing their attitudes toward the opposite sex; thus, their opinions toward Edna (TA) and Nora (ADH) were different, less stereotypical, due to the panel activity.
- ♦ Generally, these panel discussions (for any class) can serve as excellent openings to units, especially ones involving conflicts and stereotypes.

Evaluation: Grade on quality of their 1-minute presentations.

ENGLISH LANGUAGE ARTS

Teacher: Mary Lou Boucher, Terry Gillis   *Course/Subject:* English 2

Topic: Language, literature, and writing   *Time to Complete:* 2 ELT periods

Teaching Methods: Expository, Q&A, guided practice, cooperative groups, discovery, journal writing

Materials: Doris Lessing's *Through the Tunnel*, student journals

Objectives: The student will identify and use literary terms in their discussion and writing about literature. The student will use the personal experience of goal-setting to help analyze the main character.

Procedure:	*Minutes:*
Day 1	
All of us set goals. What are some goals that you have had for yourself? What are some goals that you have for yourself right now? In your journals, state one goal that you have for yourself and then list *three* things that you need to do to reach that goal.	5–10
We're going to read is *Through the Tunnel*. Watch for how the main character achieves his goal and be ready to evaluate what he does. Also watch for two of the fictional elements we brainstormed yesterday: atmosphere and character. (Quick oral check for meaning and understanding of terms.)	
Presentation—In-class reading of *Through the Tunnel* by Doris Lessing with modeling of use of details to develop setting and atmosphere. (An in-class reading would be done for the opportunity of modeling.)	20
Activity: Think, Write, Pair, Square—Individually, students think, then list what Jerry (main character) did to achieve his goal. Students respond to questions prepared by teachers.	5–10
Compass Buddy—Together consider the pros and cons of Jerry's decision. Have buddies sum up their view and report back to each one's team, using ROUND ROBIN format.	10
Guided Practice—Atmosphere. Student's name the five senses and use a graphic organizer to find three examples of details or images from the story that appeal to each of the five senses. Students begin editing and expanding a short paragraph, adding sensory details and images to create an atmosphere. This will be a writing for the writing portfolio that will be due at the end of the course.	15
Closure—Setting goals, Jerry's strategies, and your own goals. Tomorrow a story about a man in a deadly conflict. To win, he must set some goals and plan his strategy.	15
Enrichment—to be given before closure, if time—To James," poem on audiocassette about a different mother/son relationship. Poem is also in student books for them to follow along.	

Procedure:	*Minutes:*

Day 2

Remember how Jerry reached his goal of swimming through the tunnel. Let's review the steps. How do you think you would prepare for a natural disaster? What are natural disasters? Give some examples. Make a list.	5–10
The story *Leningen Versus the Ants*—Leningen has a larger goal, to save his plantation in Brazil from marching ants. To achieve his goal, Leningen has an elaborate plan. He relies on a motto to help him achieve it. Students are to record motto in journal.	15
Introduce vocabulary to understand flora and fauna story. Students will do worksheets to reinforce same.	15–20
Teacher will read aloud the story to p. 46 and ask questions regarding impending disaster, atmosphere, and goal setting. Level or reading is more difficult than previous story.	15–20
Class will set up journal for Leningen's goal according to day, goals, and reactions of him and others. A sample handout will be given. In addition, students will be recording samples of atmosphere and sensory description.	
Depending on the reading ability of the students, they will be assigned to do the remainder of the reading at home. It may be broken into several sections over two nights.	
Guided Practice—In groups have class compare notes on steps to achieving goal of protecting plantation and how ants continued to present problems. Have one member of each group put stems on board by Day 1, Group 1, Day 2, Group 2, etc.	15
Evaluation: Essay—The setting is a major obstacle to achieving goals in *Through the Tunnel* and *Leningen Versus the Ants*. Show how each character overcame nature in a step-by-step process using his brain. Brainstorm first.	60 (may span over 2 days)

ENGLISH LANGUAGE ARTS

Teacher: Robert McGee   *Course/Subject:* American Literature
Topic: Developing inquiring minds   *Time to Complete:* 1 ELT period

Teaching Methods: Socratic method combined with writing and interviews
Materials: Shirley Jackson's *The Lottery* and Robert Frost's *Mending Wall*
Objectives: Students will demonstrate critical thinking by replacing outworn traditions in an examination of literature and life with their own interpretations.

Procedure:	*Minutes:*
Students are assigned to read the Shirley Jackson's provocative short story *The Lottery* before they come to class. This story always stimulates a class through its shocking nature. We begin the class with an examination of the story. Some of the questions raised are: Why did these people participate in this event? Why is the story so shocking and how does she develop this sense of shock? Could this really happen? What is the meaning of the story? Eventually the students realize what happens when a tradition or a life is unexamined.	15–20 (discussion)
This discussion can be followed by a 15–20 minute film if it is available. The film does a good job of reinforcing the meaning of the story.	15–20
Then we turn to Frost's classic poem about accepting or questioning an existing tradition. I go over what is happening in the poem and try to make them realize that the two people in the poem, the narrator and his neighbor, represent two different ways of looking at reality.	15 (analysis & explication)
Next I have them write an essay, illustrating the similarities found in the two literary works. This way they develop critical thinking skills and realized how similar ideas can be expressed by different authors in different forms of literature.	15
Next I have them work in pairs and give them this exercise: One student writes at the top of his/her paper a choice of career. Then he or she must give a reason for that choice. The student's partner is involved in asking questions based upon that statement. Each time a question is answered, the answer engenders a new question such as "Why do you want to make a lot of money?"	15
Students will eventually realize that they have not thought a great deal about this subject or other subjects, and that they are only giving stock responses.	5 (summing up & assigning essay)
Following this I go around the room, and ask them to develop questions that are difficult to answer. Why are blackboards black or are they? Why doesn't Dick Clark ever age? Why must parents continually remind their offspring about how difficult their youth was? Why can't you pull off the tag on the mattress?	
For homework each student will write a two-page paper that attempts to answer one of these questions, and hopefully the student will realize that "the unexamined life is not worth living."	

Evaluation: The paper dealing with the intriguing question will be used to evaluate the process.

HISTORY AND SOCIAL SCIENCE

Teacher: Richard Alves   *Course/Subject:* Government

Grade Level: Secondary (9-12)   *Time to Complete:* 1 ELT period

Teaching Methods: Cooperative group learning, Q&A, guided practice

Materials: Textbooks, notebook or log book, multimedia computer system (Pentium with at least 24Mb RAM), Microsoft PowerPoint presentation program, headphones (if desired)

Objectives: This activity focuses on political parties in the United States, how they impact government policy, and the role that citizens play in the political process.

Learning Outcomes: Curriculum: The student will: **Minutes:**

♦ Describe how political ideologies lead to the formation of citizen advocacy groups.

♦ Demonstrate how political parties are organized at all levels.

♦ Explain how political parties select candidates for public office at all levels.

♦ Identify ways that political parties impact the operation of government.

Prerequisites: Team-building exercises, reading and discussion of textbook material, and student understanding of computer program operations

Procedures:

♦ Review team concept philosophy.   5

♦ Review classroom rules regarding cooperative learning activities   5

♦ Assign 1 group to each computer; if only 1 computer is available, then students must be reminded that time is of the essence.   5

♦ The group(s) using the computer proceed as the program is self-directed, the activity should take no more than 30 minutes.   30

♦ Groups not using the computer will work cooperatively on preassigned tasks (e.g., readings, worksheets, teacher/group conferencing, etc.).   10

♦ When a group has completed the multimedia activity they will immediately conference with the teacher for a debriefing session.   15

♦ Each group follows in turn until all students have had the opportunity to complete the assignment.

♦ Upon finishing the multimedia activity the group begins to work on their "Extension Activity."

Closure Activities:

♦ The class will come together as a whole to carry out their "extension activities" as previously assigned.   20

♦ The class will discuss answers to the computer activity questions.

♦ The teacher will complete log book assignments.

Evaluation: Teacher debriefing session, written assignments (log books) are checked, individual queries by the teacher (oral), and written test.

HISTORY AND SOCIAL

Teacher: Joseph Brucato   *Course/Subject:* European History
Topic: Protestant Reformation   *Time to Complete:* 1 ELT period

Teaching Methods: Role play, simulation, discussion, critical thinking, and writing

Materials: Textbook, notes

Objectives: Students will demonstrate knowledge and understanding of the Protestant Reformation.

	Minutes:
Procedure: Students will create, imagine, simulate, and/or role play an historical event, an individual, or situation related to the Protestant Reformation.	

Presentation:

Students are given a short passage to read regarding the problems of the Catholic Church.	5
Students are given a short passage about the life and beliefs of Martin Luther.	5
The class engages in a discussion that outlines several controversies and problems related to the Catholic Church in the Middle Ages (simony, nepotism, indulgences, etc.)	15–20
The class is divided into groups of 3–5 students with each group being assigned a different task:	5
• Group 1: Each student contributes to a diary or journal assuming the role of Martin Luther (i.e., his life, views, hopes and fears).	30 (per group)
• Group 2: Creates a satirical cartoon that lampoons the controversy between the Catholic and Protestant Churches.	
• Group 3: Creates a dialogue in which the pope, a bishop, and a parish priest debate a Protestant minister on the laws and rules of their respective churches.	
• Group 4: Creates an original skit with at least three characters and the theme of "The Inquisition."	
A spokesperson from each group describes the outcome of the group activity to the entire class. The teacher moderates the Q&A from the remainder of the class.	10
Each group reconvenes to consider the reactions from the other groups and modifies or completes their projects.	5
Each group reports any changes to their final projects.	5

Evaluation: Group projects, individual contributions to class.

HISTORY AND SOCIAL SCIENCE

Teacher: John Daigle *Course/Subject:* Economics

Topic: Interest rates and inverse relation- *Time to Complete:* 1 ELT period
ships

Teaching Methods: Expository, Q&A, and cooperative group learning

Materials: None necessary

Objectives: Students will demonstrate an understanding of the inverse relationship between interest rates and stock market values.

Procedure:	*Minutes:*
The teacher will present an introductory lecture on inverse relationships. As part of the lecture, the teacher will ask students to give examples of inverse relationships that exist in daily life. Discussions will follow and will conclude when students have demonstrated a fundamental understanding of the concept.	20
Students will divided into groups of 3–5 students and asked to discuss and conclude how higher interest rates would affect the following:	20

- Group 1—What they buy
- Group 2—What their parents buy
- Group 3—What a corporation might buy
- Group 4—What the government buys
- Group 5—Where people would place their savings

The teacher will circulate and monitor the progress of individual students and group activities.	
Each group will present a report of its findings to the class	20
Each group will reconvene and evaluate the effect its findings would likely have on the price of stocks (i.e., why they would likely fall and how) demonstrating an inverse relationship	10
Each group will present a report of its deliberations to the class	10
Closing discussion of the lesson will follow the group presentations	5

Evaluation: Written group reports, group projects, and individual written test.

HISTORY AND SOCIAL SCIENCE

Teacher: Kevin Maines   *Course/Subject:* U.S. History

Topic: A study of the Chicago 8 and William *Time to Complete:* 4 ELT periods
Calley trials and how they impacted
American society and its legal system.

Teaching Methods: Expository, Q&A, guided practice, cooperative groups, discovery, journal writing

Materials: Primary and secondary source reading materials, access to library resources, the Electronic Library, and the Internet. This lesson will also require case study materials, HBO's movie "Conspiracy; The Chicago 8 Trial," a television documentary on the year 1968, a television documentary on the Democratic National Convention of 1968, and the BBC documentary "Four Hours in My Lai."

Objectives: The students will demonstrate understanding of the short story literary terms in reading, writing and discussion. In a brief review of previous story, students will review motivation and goal setting to lead into story with similar theme and characterization but in a more highly developed literary work.

Procedure:	*Minutes:*
The students will be divided into four groups so as to represent the prosecution and defense teams for both cases.	2–3
The students will elect a lead attorney for their group who will be responsible for organizing and assigning responsibilities for each group member.	2–3
The students will research their case through their textbook, case study book, law reference books, print media, and professional journals that are on the Electronic Library and at appropriate (teacher-supervised searches) Internet sites; take their readings and prepare an outline/ overview of the important information as it pertains to their case; and, present their information to the group. Through discussion, the group will decide what information from the presentation will be used in preparing their legal brief.	75–80
The students will begin preparing their legal arguments, which will be presented in the form of opening arguments. All members contribute to this written brief by being responsible for their content area and its inclusion into the brief. The group must prepare an opening statement that covers the criminal issues of the case, any constitutional issues involved in the case, and all legal issues that need to be addressed in their case.	30
Then they refine their opening arguments to make sure that the arguments are inclusive of all important and relevant materials. They should also refine the sequence of the information that they are going to present.	15
The students will rehearse the presentation of their opening statement. They will need to use the classroom as a courtroom and be sure that they are projecting their voice and speaking in a tone that reflects confidence and knowledge. Each member of the group will be expected to present some information to the class during the opening statements. This will need to be rehearsed so the transitions are smooth.	40

Procedure:	*Minutes:*

The students will present their opening arguments to the class. The class-room will be converted into a courtroom. Each group of attorneys will have an area designated for them. The teacher or a student will serve as judge and be seated in an area designated for him/her. The students will be expected to stand and move about the courtroom while making their presentation. They can use note cards but should not rely totally on them. The judge can stop the presentation if he/she feels that an important point needs greater clarity or emphasis. **20**

The students will have to field directed questions from their adversaries on points of law or legal concerns raised in the cases. This should spark an ongoing debate on the cases. The judge must facilitate this debate and keep it focused on the subject matter. The teacher should also have prepared a number of questions for each group to respond to that will direct the class toward achieving an understanding of the cases. It is important that all feel free to express their ideas and not to feel inhibited or intimidated by anyone. Those students who are not actively involved on the panel should feel free to ask questions and to engage in the debate on the cases. **20**

On completion of the opening arguments and debate, both groups will retire to prepare their closing arguments. These should have been cre-ated prior to this time and now should undergo a modification based on the points raised during questioning and debate. The closing argu-ments must reflect the important points that were made during the opening statements and debate, and should reflect a compassionate appeal for the court to rule in its favor. **10**

The students then present their closing arguments to the court. This should involve as many participants as possible and should be fo-cused on convincing the judge and jury to rule in their favor. **10**

The audience, which has served as a jury, will be asked to write their de-cision on a secret ballot and pass it to the judge. The decision of the jury will be read to the courtroom by the judge. **15**

The students then take notes from a brief lecture by the teacher on the key legal and historical points of the case presented. **15**

The students will be asked to take an objective test on the cases. **70**

The students will have an opportunity to grade each group's perfor-mance based on the accuracy of material that was presented and how convincing the group was during its presentation. They will also be asked as a group to grade their own group's performance and to grade the work of each member of the groups performance. The rubric will have been determined in advance of the presentations as part of the in-troduction. Some student input in determining the rubric is permitted. **15**

Evaluation: Observation and evaluation of research materials for rele-vance to subject, in-class presentation, checking for understanding through questioning during the entire process, establishment of a grading rubric and evaluation of written responses to open-ended es-say question on an examination.

HISTORY AND SOCIAL SCIENCE

Teacher: Beth Fusco   *Course/Subject:* World Studies 1
Topic: Ancient China   *Time to Complete:* 85 minutes

Teaching Methods: Expository, cooperative groups

Materials: World studies text book

Objectives: This lesson is designed to introduce students to ancient China and to create an overview of the geographical, political, and philosophical influences that form the basis of the Chinese culture and civilization. This lesson will produce a 1-page chart summary that will be used as the basis for future lessons. The chart will identify the concepts requiring further elaboration and provide a tool to analyze China on a cause/effect and compare/contrast basis. Using a collaborative method, each student will research, take notes, and share information. This lesson also reinforces the skill of extracting key facts and condensing notes.

Procedure:	*Minutes:*
Teacher will solicit student ideas and understanding of China by asking them to write 5 things that they associate with China. The teacher will compile their ideas on the board and state that we will try to uncover the historical facts that support the things or beliefs they've identified.	5
Introduce the time period and the three areas that will be explored: geographical, political, and philosophical influences. Define "philosophical" influences and solicit what they think they will learn within each area, making connections between broad topics and the type of supporting facts associated with them.	5
Explain that each student will be given a specific area to research. Randomly pass out one of the sections to each student. (There are eight sections and typically 3–4 students will be doing the same section). Read the instructions of the lesson.	5
Each student will research their section using the text book, answer the questions in full sentences, then transfer their notes to their master sheet using brief bullet points.	20
Students switch their top sheet with a person who needs their section and who has a section they need. Each student keeps their own master chart and transfers information from their classmate's top sheet to their master chart (condensing the information from full sentences to brief points.). They now use the cover page they received to switch with the next person. Continue this until each student has a completed chart.	30
When their master chart is complete, pair them into 8 small groups to compare master charts. Students will add anything they do not have to their chart.	5
Evaluation: Verbally quiz students regarding notes, charts, key concepts, and discussion, or students can use their notes to write a summary either individually, in groups, or as a class on the board.	15

MATHEMATICS

Teacher: Maryanne Boberg
Course/Subject: SAT Math Review
Topic: Review of angle relationships, team building
Time to Complete: 45 minutes

Teaching Methods: Cooperative groups, Q&A
Materials: Lettered Heads, Angle Web
Objectives:

♦ Students will become familiar with other members of their newly formed teams.
♦ Students will determine their own background regarding angle relations.

Procedure:	*Minutes:*

Part 1: Students are seated in teams of 4 so that there is 1 high-level, 2 medium-level, and 1 low-level student on each team. Consideration is also given to having a good girl/boy mix.   20

Activity 1: Lettered Heads
• Each student in the team will select a letter—A, B, C, or D.
• Each person will be asked to respond to a question after consulting with his/her team members and report the answers for all members to the class and teacher.
• The questions:
  ▪ Person A will reorport the answers to this question: "*name of student* took Geometry with *name of teacher* <u>when</u>."
  ▪ Person B will report: "*student's name* liked/disliked Geometry because _____"
  ▪ Person C will report: "Something that *name of student* remembers about angles is _____"
  ▪ Person D will rept: "If *student's name* were a Geometric shape, he/she would be a _____ because _____"

Part 2: Web activity using the student-generated responses to Question #3.   20

• The teacher will write all responses from each team on the board in the form of a web (right or wrong, exactly as reported by students)
• After all teams have reported, the teacher will review the facts and challenge the class to find any that are unclear, incorrect, or misleading so that they can be corrected and/or amended. Ex. Alternate interior angles are congruent. This must be amended to include ONLY when two PARALLEL lines are cut by a transversal.

Homework: Worksheets on angle relations are distributed   1

Evaluation: Questions #1 and #2 provide the class and teacher with a quick background and attitude for each student; question #3 is the content information for the review (facts are listed on the web so that the teacher can assess the level of understanding for the class); question #4 is included to add humor and fun to the activity.

MATHEMATICS

Teacher: Alan DiFonzo   *Course/Subject:* Discrete Math

Topic: Depth-first search   *Time to Complete:* 1 ELT period

Teaching Methods: Discovery

Materials: Various maps of sections of the town

Objectives: Students will demonstrate a knowledge of the depth-first search algorithm, the Hamiltonian cycle, and a minimal spanning tree.

Procedure:	*Minutes:*

Describe the overview of the problems related to this unit. These problems can be completed by pairs or groups of three students. The teacher serves as a facilitator to the group activities   10

Determine if a one-way road system can be developed for your town by following these directions: 20

- Draw a graph based on the road map. The vertices will represent the intersections of the streets and the edges will be the streets.
- Label the vertices with capital letters starting with A. Then use the depth-first algorithm to numerically label the vertices starting at vertex A.
- Place the appropriate arrow on the tree edges and list the tree edges.
- Place the appropriate arrow on the back edges and list the back edge.
- Is it possible to develop a one-way road system in your town? Explain.
- Would it still be possible to develop this road system if an entire street was traveled in the same direction? Explain.

You are in charge of developing a bus route through the streets of your town. Determine if it is possible to route the bus through the town so that it begins and ends at vertex A; in addition, no child must walk more than half a block to an intersection to get on the bus. If this is not possible, then determine the best route with this condition in mind. Using graph theory terminology, what are you trying to develop? Explain.   20

Electricity has just been discovered and your town wants to install a street light at each intersection. Funds, however, are limited and this must be done in the most economical manner possible. Use the numerical value on each street as the cost in hundreds of dollars for stringing the wire along each street between intersections. Starting at vertex A determine the minimal cost for this project. Using graph theory terminology, what are you trying to develop? Explain.   20

Groups of students explain their respective answers to the questions posed and their rationale.   15

Evaluation: Evaluations of individual problems and contributions to the group process.

MATHEMATICS

Teacher: Carol Fiedler   *Course/Subject:* Trigonometry
Topic: Law of Sines   *Time to Complete:* 80–86 minutes

Teaching Methods: Review, assess, inspect, conclude, develop

Materials: Worksheet, blackboard, calculators

Objectives: Students will demonstrate their knowledge of the Law of Sines by introducing multiple and/or nonexistent answers to triangle problems.

Procedure:	*Minutes:*

After introducing Law of Sines and completing two sets of problems, students will be exposed to the possibility of a nonunique solution to problems.

• Review problems with Law of Sines.	10–15
• Quiz given on Law of Sines to determine proficiency.	15–25
• Review types of triangles that cannot be solved by using Law of Sines (from previous assignment).	5–10
• Place three problems on the board and ask students to solve using Law of Sines. One problem has exactly one solution, one has no solution, and one has two different solutions.	10–15
• Students discuss in groups why each problem had the solutions listed above. The class then brainstorms reasons why and tries to come up with a method to determine the number of solutions.	10–15
• After making a general algorithm to determine the number of solutions, students examine several problems and make an educated guess about the solution to each problem. Then they do the practice exercises. There are 6 different problems; each student is assigned 2–3; then they partner with other students who have done these problems and discuss results.	10–15
• The students then amend the algorithm as needed. Appropriate problems are assigned for homework (at end of period)	

Evaluation: Quiz (see #2); group evaluation of use of algorithm; experimentation to see if algorithm is correct or needs to be amended.

• Quiz on Law of Sines
• Brainstorming ideas
• Checking with partner on practice exercises
• Homework due next day

MATHEMATICS

Teacher: Jean Newcomb, Lorraine Tumolo   *Course/Subject:* Pre-Calculus and pos-
Topic: Trigonometric graphing   sibly Trigonometry
                                                                     Time to Complete: 1.5 ELT periods

Teaching Methods: Group Activity; Self-Discovery

Materials: Graphing calculator, large index cards

Objectives: Students will demonstrate:

♦ The use of technology to develop the basic graphs of $y = \tan x$, $y = \cot x$, $y = \sec x$, and $y = \csc x$.

♦ Comprehension of these new functions extends their previous knowledge of reflection, vertical and horizontal stretching and shrinking, and translations of graphs.

Procedure:	*Minutes:*

♦ Guided self-discovery within a cooperative learning environment   60
using graphing calculators. Questions 1–8.

Ex: Using the graphing calculator in radian mode and ztrig, graph
the following functions. Sketch your graphs on the axes provided
labeling both axes with appropriate scale values:
$$Y1 = \sin x$$
$$Y2 = 1/\sin x \text{ or } y = (\sin x)\text{-}1$$

♦ Paragraph writing. Question 9.

Ex: Write a paragraph to explain why it does not make sense to talk   5
about the amplitudes of these new graphs.

♦ Extend previous knowledge. Questions 10–19.   15
                                                                                                              (Assign as
Ex: Match each function in problems #10–19 with the letter of its   homework)
corresponding graph. State the period of each function.

♦ Open-ended question. Question 20.   30

Ex: Without using the graphing calculator, determine two equations like those in the matching exercises above. Graph at least one period of these equations with clearly marked scaling on the axes.

♦ Additional practice, group activity. Question 21. Summarize with discussion.

Ex: Exchange cards with at least three other groups in the classroom. Write below the group number and the questions you found for their graphs.

Evaluation: Choose one packet from each group and assign a group grade.

MATHEMATICS

Teacher: Wayne Tanson, John Vasta   *Course/Subject:* Pre-Algebra/Algebra 1
Topic: Simplifying numerical expressions *Time to Complete:* 1 ELT period

Teaching Methods: Guided practice, discussion, hands-on activities, cooperative pairs

Materials: TI-85 calculators

Objectives: Students will be able to simplify numerical expressions and evaluate algebraic expressions on paper using the order of operations and the TI-85.

Procedure:	*Minutes:*
Check homework; have students put teacher-selected problems on the chalkboard; i.e., have students simplify the expressions such as $$3+3/3+7-6+2+5^2-(4+3)$$	15
Solicit responses from students regarding their answers to the expressions (there should be a number of different responses). Explain that there must be an order of operations so that everyone gets the same answer to a problem. Write notes on "Order of Operations" with examples on the chalkboard.	20
Break class into "compass pairs" for guided-practice problems; demonstrate how to use the TI-85 to check answers. Teacher checks student progress.	20
Discussion of class work to check for understanding. Students should verify their answers using the TI-85.	5
Have students evaluate an expression (e.g., x^2-3x+3 for $x=-2$). Review by continuing guided practice activities.	10
Switch "compass pair" direction and complete additional problems as the teacher circulates checking for understanding.	15
Closure: Make real world connections with the problems the students have been working on and assign homework.	5

Evaluation: Class participation, journal entries, homework, quizzes and tests, and notebook.

SCIENCE AND TECHNOLOGY

Teacher: Jennifer Carr *Course/Subject:* Biology
Topic: Protein synthesis *Time to Complete:* 1 ELT period

Teaching Methods: Discussion, physical modeling of process

Materials: Colored cardboard pieces of DNA, mRNA, tRNA, amino acid "words," pieces of white paper, pen or marker, and tape.

Objectives: Students will be able demonstrate their understanding of protein synthesis within the cell.

Procedure:	*Minutes:*
Review or preview the functions of DNA, mRNA, tRNA, and ribosomes in protein synthesis; remind students that they will be modeling the process with paper and by acting out the roles involved.	20
Designate tables/desk groups in the room to be the following areas inside a cell: the nucleus, the ER with ribosomes, and the "empty" space left to be the cell cytoplasm, and introduce the paper molecules.	5
Assign each student a partner and get a DNA strip to decode. Students will then find:	20

- The complementary mRNA codons to match their DNA strip and tape these together.
- The complementary tRNA molecules (with anticondons) to their mRNA strip.
- Finally, each tRNA is a particular color of cardboard paper. Students must keep their tRNA in the right order and match their amino acid word by color to it. If the student has completed this exercise correctly, the pieces will spell out a sentence that makes sense.

Students will then discuss how this modeling process is similar or dissimilar to the process of protein synthesis that occurs in the cell.	20

- Similarities: DNA stays in the nucleus, mRNA leaves, matching the DNA to codons then anticodons; protein synthesis takes place outside the nucleus at ribosomes; each tRNA has a specific amino acid it matches with, etc.
- Differences: Absence of stop and start codons, the tRNA in the cell attach to their amino acid before reaching the ribosome, absence of the "A" and "P" spaces in the ribosome, etc.

Divide students into small groups and give each group a sample DNA strip. Each group must choose a role, make a sign for themselves and design codon cards of mRNA to match their DNA strip. They must also design amino acid words to make a sentence. One person can be the ribosome, one person the nucleus, one person carries the mRNA message, and the rest are tRNAs and amino acids. Each group acts out protein synthesis in front of the class and produces a protein sentence.	20

Evaluation: Each student writes a journal entry describing the protein synthesis process

SCIENCE AND TECHNOLOGY

Teacher: Bill Gary   *Course/Subject:* Physics
Topic: Hooke's Law   *Time to Complete:* 1 ELT period

Teaching Methods: Directed instruction, demonstration, small group activities, and laboratory experience

Materials: Textbook, graph paper, ruler, spring (with apparatus will save time), gram/newton scale, various gram masses, something to hang the springs from The teacher will need a guitar that uses a spring-balanced floating bridge such as the design employed by Fender Stratocaster guitars. Guitars that have fixed bridges (bridges that are glued or screwed down to the guitar body) will not do here.

Objectives: The student will demonstrate an understanding of Hooke's Law by synthesize components of class problems, directed instruction, and lab work into a meaningful lab experience.

Procedure:	*Minutes:*
Directed instruction will focus upon a force and elongation graph where the y-axis (force) and the x-axis (elongation) represented by the equation	10

$$Y = mx + b \text{ (where the force is a constant)}$$

Demonstrate the construction of a guitar as it relates to physics and music (i.e., how the construction helps a musician achieve different sounds, how the various components can be used to create false harmonics, how the springs attached to the floating bridge stretch and contract as the trem arm is pulled just like the problems in a textbook, how springs can keep constant tension on the strings and the neck of the guitar, how the different diameter strings and various tensions produce different sounds, etc.). Students discover via Q&A that to find the work being done by the guitar, they must find the area under the graph by finding the area of a triangle, that the force needed to pull a spring (fixed at one end) is directly proportional to the displacement of the spring.	20

$$\text{Area} = \tfrac{1}{2}kx^2 \text{ (the work)}$$

Students enter the lab component of this lesson to demonstrate Hooke's Law. The teacher monitors individual and group laboratory work, asks prompting questions, etc.	45
Students complete their lab reports.	10

Evaluation: Classroom participation and laboratory reports.

SCIENCE AND TECHNOLOGY

Teacher: Louis Piazza   *Course/Subject:* Chemistry
Topic: Equilibrium   *Time to Complete:* 3 ELT periods

Teaching Methods: Expository, cooperative, Q&A, discovery

Materials: Acids, bases, salts—spectrophotometer—conductivity tester

Objectives: Upon completing this series of lessons students will be able to define chemical equilibrium, explain the nature of the equilibrium constant, write chemical equations and perform calculations involving the equilibrium constant, discuss factors that disturb equilibrium, discuss conditions under which reactions go to completion, describe the common ion effect, develop skill of using the spectrophotometer, and observe factors that affect equilibrium.

Procedure:	*Minutes:*

Day 1

• Teacher will demonstrate reactions of acids and bases with indicators as examples of reversible reactions.	10
• Class discussion of above reactions from an equilibrium perspective.	25
• Teacher will explain Hydrogen Iodide equilibrium and work a sample problem.	15
• Students will work practice problems in groups.	20
• Teacher and students will begin pre-lab for experiment Determining Equilibrium Constant.	15

Day 2

• Teacher and students will engage in pre-lab discussion. Safety and accuracy will be emphasized.	10
• Students will perform experiment in groups of two. Teacher will assist.	60
• Post lab discussion of results.	15

Day 3

• Students will view the Chem Study Video *Molecules in Action.* Teacher will stop video periodically (5–7 min. max.) for discussion.	30
• Teacher will demonstrate shifting equilibrium. Class will discuss results and apply LeChatalier's Principle.	20
• Students will work in groups on practice problems. Teacher will circulate and assist.	35

Evaluation: Students will be evaluated using the following criteria:

- Student's participation in the class discussions.
- Student's observation of proper lab techniques and procedures.
- Student's written formal lab report on the experiment.
- Student's passing a written test on the material.

SCIENCE AND TECHNOLOGY

Teacher: Pauline Kalagher, PhD   *Course/Subject:* Biology
Topic: The cell   *Time to Complete:* 1 ELT period

Teaching Methods: Cooperative pairs, laboratory experience, guided practice

Materials: Microscope, glass slides, cover slips, toothpicks, methylene blue die, Lugol's solution, onion skin cells, student cheek cells, Elodea leaves, overhead projector, student notebooks, student textbooks, student quiz on the cell and cell organelles.

Objectives: Students will be able to state the three parts of the cell theory, distinguish between prokaryotic and eukaryotic cells, describe the relationship between cell function and cell shape, identify four differences between plant and animal cells, label the organelles found in a "typical" animal cell, and describe the major functions of the cell's organelles.

Procedure:	*Minutes:*
Working in teams of two students, the teams will carry out the following three short laboratory activities:	40

- Make slides of their own cheek cells, stain the cells with a drop of methylene blue, cover with a cover slip and examine the specimen under the microscope.
- Make a slide of onion skins, stain the cells with Lugol's solution, cover with a cover slip and examine the specimen under the microscope.
- Examine a leaf of the Elodea plant placing only a drop of water over the thin leaf to observe the cloroplasts found in plant cells.
- Note: Students should make drawings of their observations in their notebooks and label the cell boundaries and organelles.

Presentation: Students will:

- Make presentations to the entire class using an overhead projector   45
  and transparency of the cell, the components of the cell, etc.;
- Compare their labels of the drawings of the cells with the transparency and discuss differences;
- Discuss the relation between the shape of cells and their functions;
- Discuss the relation of cells to tissues, tissues to organs, and organs to organ systems;
- Differentiate between the various types of organisms that are comprised of cells (i.e., unicellular, colonial, and multicellular organisms);
- Differentiate between animal and plant cells;
- Describe the three components of the cell theory.

Evaluation: The students will be evaluated based upon the completion of the three laboratory activities, their class participation, and their score on a quiz based upon the above objectives to be given at the start of the next class period.

WORLD LANGUAGES

Teacher: Lisa Bertonazzi   *Course/Subject:* Italian 1

Topic: Gestures, art, and grammar   *Time to Complete:* 1 ELT period

Teaching Methods: Whole group instruction, small cooperative groups, individual assignments, and classroom learning centers.

Materials: 6 sets of gesture cards (numbered) with meanings, 2 sets of pictures of artist's most famous works (numbered on bulletin boards), blank index cards, young adult books featuring the life and works of Leonardo da Vinci, texts, work sheets, dialogues, video camera, blank VCR tape, table cloth and eating utensils, student-made menus, food pictures, TV and VCR with monitor

Objectives: Students will demonstrate increased proficiency in communication in the target language (oral, listening, and writing) as assessed by students and the teacher in accordance with a locally developed rubric.

Procedure:	*Minutes:*
Warm-up exercises—verbal commands and dialogues between the teacher and students	5
Dialogues—review previous lesson using dialogues that stress the vocabulary and grammar from a particular unit; this need not be a continuous dialogue for the entire time frame. By using various games, small-group and whole-group activities, Q&A, and choral and individual responses at different times throughout the ELT period, students will continue guided and independent practice while being monitored by the teacher.	35
Learning centers—are established around the room where students direct and participate in learning dialogues in groups of 4–6 students. The room is configured so that each learning center is separate from other learning centers with specific learning materials available for student use (a table with gesture cards; a table with menus, picture food, eating utensils, etc.; a table featuring culture pictures from famous artists, the architecture, etc.; a table with sample dialogues for oral and listening practice; a video center; a table retail/travel table where students buy various items, etc.) A variety of learning centers which change from time to time are established where students interact with one another; develop and write dialogues, skits, plays, etc., which are written, performed, and videotaped. The teacher constantly monitors the various groups and facilitates the transitions from one activity to another.	40

Evaluation: At the end of each unit, a written, oral, and listening exam is given. Each unit is based on students performing certain conversationally based activities in the target language which can be videotaped and critiqued by both students and the teacher.

WORLD LANGUAGES

Teacher: Fran Olano, Teresa A. Nelson   *Course/Subject:* Spanish 4

Topic: Giving commands (knowledge of subjunc- *Time to Complete:* 1 ELT period
tive forms), increasing the use of vocabulary,
discussion of social and ecological issues and
solutions

Teaching Methods: Didactic instruction, group work, Q&A, individual and group
work, oral presentations

Materials:

- Vocabulary lists of vocabulary of the house, chores, as well as ecology vocabulary and expressions.
- Short stories, readings, and articles on social issues to be addressed.
- Review sheets on formation of commands and subjunctive.

Objectives: Students will be able to discuss household chores and make a presentation about a parent/child discussion on the responsibility of chores.

Procedure:	*Minutes:*
◆ Students will receive vocabulary packets which will be reviewed by the teacher, especially idiomatic expressions or special verb forms.	10
◆ Students will be involved in paired interviews, discussing household chores and whose responsibility these are, and any pertinent gender roles.	15
◆ The teacher will review the formation of commands. Students will receive study sheets.	10
◆ Students will do a worksheet on the use of commands which will be reviewed with the teacher.	15
◆ Students will listen to the audiocassette *Cantos y Ritmos,* a rap tape. The rap tape focuses on the use of commands. The students will repeat the rap song 2 or 3 times. The teacher will provide a copy of the song with blanks to be filled in as the students listen to the tape.	10
◆ Students will begin to prepare presentations in groups of two. The presentation will be a discussion/disagreement between a parent/child, the giving of commands, the complaints that follow, and the ensuing discussion. The presentation, which will last 2–3 minutes, will be written and corrected by the teacher. The students will then learn their lines and make their presentations to the class at a later date.	25

Homework:

- Continue preparation of the presentation
- Write 10 sentences using commands and the vocabulary presented in class.

Evaluation: Oral presentations in the Spanish and written assignments that align with the various strands in the curriculum frameworks and established scoring rubrics.

WORLD LANGUAGES

Teacher: Mike Turner   *Course/Subject:* Conversational Spanish

Topic: Verb "gustar"—to like, to be pleas- *Time to Complete:* 1 ELT period
   ing

Teaching Methods: Guided practice, modeling, word game, and recitation

Materials: Text, video, worksheets, chalkboard, reading selection, Spanish-English
   dictionary

Objectives: Students will demonstrate proficiency in the use of the verb gustar during oral and written activities

Procedure:	*Minutes:*
Begin class with warm up greetings in Spanish, teacher-to-student exchanges, then have student-to-student exchanges.	5
Distribute worksheets with "gustar" statements that are associated with pictures, half in the affirmative and half in the negative.	10–15
Guided practice—the teacher will describe what each sentence means in English, have the students state the sentence in Spanish, and have the students write the sentences in Spanish on the worksheet.	10
Vocabulary building exercises—distribute worksheets containing squares; the teacher will ask questions in Spanish regarding the pictures in each square; students will respond in Spanish using the various forms of the verb "gustar" in their respones. New vocabulary terms will be introduced.	10
Distribute worksheets with 10–12 regular "ar" verbs associated with pictures; the teacher will describe what each sentence means in English, have the students state the sentence in Spanish, and have the students write the sentences in Spanish on the worksheet.	20
Students engage in a short reading stressing the use of the verb "gustar."	10
Have students engage in some type of competitive word game based upon the use of the verb "gustar."	10
Assign homework and monitor individual work by students as they begin their written homework assignments.	10

Evaluation: Monitoring of individual student seat work and the oral
   interactions with other students, responses to questions, choral responses, and oral presentations during various exercises.

PRACTICAL ARTS

Teacher: Bob Dwyer   *Course/Subject:* Computer Applications
Topic: Introduction to spreadsheets   *Time to Complete:* 1 ELT Period

Teaching Methods: Directed instruction, guided practice, modeling

Materials: Computer hardware, software

Objectives: The students will demonstrate:

- An understanding of what a spreadsheet is;
- Knowledge of the numeric keypad on the keyboard;
- Differentiation of rows and columns in a spreadsheet;
- Introduction of cells including empty, active, occupied, consecutive, adjacent, and random;
- Spreadsheet construction including headings and labels, expanded cells and spillage; and,
- Entering text as labels and headings and entering numeric data as values.

Procedure:	*Minutes:*

All instruction will be delivered through short, directed instruction   20
followed by guided "hands-on" activities shadowing what is being
discussed. Upon completion of this short introduction, students
will create their first spreadsheet called "Fruit."

Methodology:

Through the creation of a spreadsheet called Fruit the students will   65
experience all the necessary criteria involved in creating and inputting text and values into a spreadsheet. Students will work on their
own creating this spreadsheet at their computer, while the instructor circulates the classroom offering individual instruction and
help.

The ELT is well suited for this activity; in the past it has taken two periods to complete this lesson. The exercise of keying the spreadsheet Fruit is very long, with much repetition. Upon the completion of this spreadsheet the student is well-acquainted and is at
ease with the task of creating a spreadsheet.

Followup:

This spreadsheet will be used again during the next class to introduce
the concept of writing formulas, specifically the plus formula.

Spreadsheet development is a two-fold process: (1) inputting of text
and values and (2) the writing of formulas, better known as
"crunching the numbers."

Evaluation: The evaluation of this lesson is based on the student's accuracy in the two-fold process.

PRACTICAL ARTS

Teacher: Dennis J. Candini   *Course/Subject:* Keyboarding

Topic: Learning correct keyboarding technique   *Time to Complete:* 22 ELT classes

Teaching Methods: Teacher direction, demonstration, and supervision of students performing hands-on activities.

Materials: Computer hardware, software, and keyboarding textbook.

Objectives: Student will demonstrate keying from printed copy while using proper touch technique.

Main Goals: Effective utilization of available time within an Extended Learning Period to provide a constructive learning experience for students learning proper keyboarding technique.

Learning proper keyboarding technique is a student-centered activity that requires a combination of teacher-directed instruction along with a great deal of individual guided practice. Not all students will develop the skill at the same pace, but all students must respond to the instruction with concentration and self-discipline to progress at an appreciable level. The teacher must closely manage, monitor, and provide positive reinforcement to the class not only as a group, but also individually, to achieve maximum performance by all.

Following is a template designed for the presentation of new keys and the review of keys already learned. The instructor can apply the ranges of time listed according to the group's performance during the early critical stages of developing proper keyboarding technique.

During guided-practice time it is important to allow students time to absorb current keys prior to beginning more new keys or students can easily become frustrated and stray from proper technique. In a heterogeneous group, there will most likely be varying levels of ability that could also affect student learning.

Procedure:

After booting up computer and preparing to type, the student will key review exercises followed by teacher presentation of new keys and related guided practice.

Activity:	*Minutes:*
♦ Students bootup computer and prepare to type.	3–5
♦ Students key a review oriented "conditioning practice" selected by the teacher at their own pace followed by the teacher dictating drills involving keys already learned.	5–8
♦ While utilizing a wall chart of the keyboard, new keys are presented, technique is demonstrated, and related drills are dictated by the teacher.	5–8
♦ The teacher supervises guided-practice wherein students key exercises emphasizing the use of the new keys. During this time the teacher monitors the group, and, if necessary, offers group and individual suggestions based on observation.	18–22
♦ The student will review all keys learned through teacher dictation of related drills.	5–8
♦ While utilizing a wall chart of the keyboard, new keys are presented, technique is demonstrated, and related drills are dictated by the teacher.	5–8
♦ The teacher supervises guided-practice wherein students key exercises emphasizing the use of the new keys. During this time the teacher monitors the group, and if necessary, offers group and individual suggestions based on observation.	18–22
♦ The students will review all keys learned through teacher dictation of related drills.	5–8
♦ Students will close down the computer station and put materials away.	2–4

The above template could be used for learning all keys in whatever sequence the teacher desires, or as presented in a keyboarding textbook. Modifications in pace of instruction and time could be made according to the students' development of skill.

Evaluation: While students are learning touch technique, the evaluation is mainly subjective based on teacher observation. After all the keys are learned, evaluation may also include typing speed and production work.

PRACTICAL ARTS

Teacher: Pamela Hennessy   *Course/Subject:* Child Development
Topic: Nutrition   *Time to Complete:* 2 ELT periods

Teaching Methods: Lecture, small group projects/research and presentations
Materials: Texts, print material resources including magazines, graphics supplies
Objectives: Given an overview of the topic and access to resource materials, students
   will create a visual display that correctly illustrates the food pyramid. This display will highlight the appropriate number of servings for foods in each group,
   the nutritional benefits to a developing fetus, and other factors important to
   proper nutrition for pregnant women.

Procedure: **Day 1**   *Minutes:*

- The teacher will present an overview of the basic concepts for the Food   10
  Pyramid.
- Students will be divided into five small groups and each group will se-   5
  lect one food group on which it will focus.
- Using their texts and other available resource materials, including mag-   30
  azines, students working in the groups will research the structure of the
  Food Pyramid and determine the number of servings of foods in each
  group that are appropriate to the needs for both a nonpregnant and a
  pregnant woman.
- Within the groups the students will plan for the development of a   15
  means to display the results of their research.
- Individual student groups will report their plans to the teacher for ap-   35
  proval prior to proceeding with the execution of the display concept.
  Once approved, students will make arrangements to acquire the necessary materials and resources and proceed with the construction of the
  display. Students will assign individual responsibility for the various
  components of the group's display.

Note: This activity will carry over into the second day and individual student components will constitute their homework assignments for the
   next class.

Day 2

- Students, working in groups, will complete the construction of their
  group displays and they will prepare oral presentations to be delivered
  to the other class members.
- Students, working in groups involving all group members, will display
  and deliver oral presentations on their research. They will also answer
  questions from class members and the teacher regarding their displays
  and presentations.

Evaluation: Students will be evaluated as members of their respective
   groups and on their individual work.
The teacher will evaluate individual work for completeness and appropri-
   ateness with respect to the lesson objectives. Group grades will be developed from teacher evaluations of each display and its accompanying
   presentation.

PRACTICAL ARTS

Teacher: Mary Lee   *Course/Subject:* Computer Applications
Topic: Databases   *Time to Complete:* 1 ELT period

Teaching Methods: Interactive, experiential, whole learning, problem solving, listening, and reading.

Materials: Computer with appropriate software for each student.

Objectives: The student will demonstrate the ability to create a database from inception and to differentiate between design and datasheet views.

Procedure:	*Minutes:*
Introduction and discussion of the purpose and use of a database	5
The database is introduced to students through text reading, teacher clarification, and simultaneous computer application with special attention given to new vocabulary terms.	40
Students will switch to different views of the database and clarify what each view is used for. Peer-student support will be encouraged to facilitate the pace of the lesson.	
When students are comfortable with the database, they will key in a short database exercise from the text, and practice switching between the different views of the database and saving the data. A second database simulation will follow.	
A discussion of the everyday practical application of databases will center upon where do databases already have an impact on student's lives, how they can use databases in their everyday lives, and why databases are important to their futures.	35
Students will discuss the differences between a database and a spreadsheet.	
Closure: Students will save their work, print copies as necessary, and close down their databases.	5

Evaluation: Computerized application tests, self-evaluation tests, and project evaluations with accommodations for the various achievement levels of the individual students.

PRACTICAL ARTS

Teacher: Jose D. Pinto   *Course/Subject:* Desktop Publishing
Topic: Illustrating in *Corel Draw* (3D key   *Time to Complete:* 1 ELT period
   designs)

Teaching Methods: Visual presentation of the project objectives and procedure and
   individualized student projects.

Materials:

♦ Personal computer

♦ Computer projection device

♦ Written and illustrated step-by-step instructions

Objectives: The students will be able to:

♦ Identify and utilize linear shape, arrange, combine, fill, separate, and powerclip
   tool functions.

♦ Demonstrate the ability to be proficient with each tool.

♦ Follow detailed instructions and listen attentively.

♦ Develop both technical and creative skills.

♦ Design and print an illustration of several keys in three-dimensional format by
   following written and verbal instruction.

Procedure:	*Minutes:*
♦ Remind students of the proper procedure of powering the computer on and off.	
♦ Demonstrate the steps of the procedure through the use of a computer projection device.	10
♦ Have each student setup their computer (layout, margins, and design settings).	5
♦ Students will follow teacher instruction step-by-step (visual on screen) to design the first key.	20
♦ Students will follow written instruction and design a second key.	20
♦ Students will work in pairs to combine and print their key designs.	15
♦ Students will evaluate each design in group critics.	12

Evaluation:

♦ Observation during class activities.

♦ Participation in group critics

♦ Evaluation of printed project.

♦ Quiz on tool function at the next class.

FINE ARTS

Teacher: Jane Yacovone   *Course/Subject:* Crafts 1
Topic: Hologram paper quilt   *Time to Complete:* 2 ELT classes

Teaching Methods: Direct instruction, modeling, and hands-on demonstration.

Materials: Drawing paper, pencil, ruler, scissors, transfer paper, halagram paper, exacto knife, cutting board, rubber cement

Objectives: Each student will demonstrate their ability to draw a symmetrical design and to create a section for a hologram paper quilt.

Demonstration:

Introduction will include examples from Amish quilt designs and basic geometric shapes. An 8½" square will be divided into 8 sections to show how to create a symmetrical design.

Once design is obtained, the students will become aware of the changes that occur when different hologram paper is placed together. Overlapping papers can create subtle blends or drastic contrasts.

The students will be shown 2 ways to transfer their design onto the back of the hologram paper. They will choose either a transfer method using transfer carbon paper or a cutting method where a template is cut from the original design.

The cut shapes will then be glued in place with rubber cement.

Procedure: *Minutes:*

The student will design an 8½" square, symmetrical quilt design pattern.

The student will choose up to 5 different hologram papers. They will overlap the papers to create subtle or drastic contrasts before choosing paper combinations.

Students will choose 1 background paper and cut it into an 8½" square. A transfer method will be used to transfer their design to the back of the hologram paper. Paper will be cut with either scissors or an exacto knife and cutting board. Each shape will be glued down as they go along.

Once original design is completed, each student will decide if more detail could be added to enhance design.

Students individual quilt pieces will be place together to create a full size wall hanging.

Day 1	Teacher demonstration	30
	Individual student practice with teacher monitoring	45
	Cleanup	10
Day 2	Transfer	25
	Cut	25
	Paste	25
	Cleanup	10

Evaluation: The degree to which student objectives were met.

FINE ARTS

Teacher: Dan Evans   *Course/Subject:* Music Theory II
Topic: Forman elements and the phrase   *Time to Complete:* 170 minutes

Teaching Methods: Lecture, experiential learning, analysis, composition, small group interaction, presentation

Materials:

♦ Worksheets to include various examples of phrase structure. There should be examples from traditional jazz and classical idioms as well as examples that can be easily played by a first-year piano student. Melodic and harmonic structure should be clearly definable.

♦ Worksheet from a children's song book: melody line should be printed and the bass should be left blank for students to provide the harmonic progression.

♦ Piano lab with enough keyboards available for individual work. The lab should be set up to provide capability for small group interaction.

♦ Computer lab with Encore or similar music composition program.

Objectives: Given an overview of the topic and access to materials, students will demonstrate their understanding of phrasal analysis by composing and performing a 16-measure piece.

Procedure:	*Minutes:*

Day 1

♦ The teacher will provide a lecture on the basic concepts of melodic and harmonic structure of the phrase. The lecture should included written examples and demonstrations by the teacher.	30
♦ Students will move to the piano lab and work independently to locate and define phrases and phrase structures in given handouts by playing them on the piano. Students will provide proper chord accompaniment to given melodies.	30
♦ Students will begin compositions of a 16-measure melody. Upon completion, the melody should be accurately harmonized and analyzed for harmonic as well as phrasal structure.	25

Day 2

♦ Students will continue to work on composition and analysis.	20
♦ Students will split into groups of four to perform and critique compositions.	30
♦ Students will move into computer lab to enter final copy into Encore program for presentation.	35

Evaluation: The degree to which students meet the individual performance objectives.

SPECIAL EDUCATION

Teacher: Cheryl Quinn

Topic: Metric volume

Course/Subject: General Science (Resource Room Setting)

Time to Complete: 1 ELT period

Teaching Methods: Cooperative group work in a laboratory setting

Materials: (each group will need all materials)—A 2-liter plastic bottle (empty); a graduated cylinder; a beaker; 1 blank die with + and − written equally on all sides; 1 blank die with ml, dl, cl written equally on all sides; a pitcher of water; a copy of the attached worksheet on acetate; a grease pen/pencil for each group.

Objectives: The student will be able to:

♦ Identify the metric units for liquid volume (ml, cl, dl)

♦ Use a graduated cylinder and a breaker

♦ Add and subtract various volumes of a liquid

♦ Make conversions of metric volume amounts

Procedure:	*Minutes:*

Metric volume conversions review using Send-A-Problem. Students are paired using Clock Buddies charts. Each person writes a metric volume conversion problem on an index card. Both cards are reviewed and worked out by each pair for an accurate answer. When all pairs are ready, they pass their problem cards to another pair to solve. This continues until all pairs have done all cards.   **20**

"Fill-R-Up" activity introduced; procedure is demonstrated for whole class. Groups of three established using a deck of cards. Each member is assigned a job: **15**

• Roll dice
• Add or subtract water from bottle
• Make list of water added or subtracted to bottle in sequence

Materials are distributed to each group.

Both dice are rolled to determine if water is added (+) or subtracted (−) from the bottle, and what metric volume is to be added or subtracted (ml, dl, cl). A running tally is kept of each roll and the amount to be added or subtracted in sequential order. The group to fill its bottle to the top first stops the activity.   **30**

The worksheet on acetate is put on the overhead. Math calculations are completed by the entire class to verity that 2 liters of water was collected correctly. Math work is gone over for accuracy.   **10**

Write a letter to a friend explaining the activity and the importance of knowing how to do metric conversions.   **10**

Evaluation: The group that fills their bottle first, and has accurate conversions totaling 2 liters, WINS, and each member receives 5 points on the upcoming metric conversions test. The letters are graded as a journal entry.

SPECIAL EDUCATION

Teacher: Cheryl Quinn   *Course/Subject:* General Science
Topic: Scientific method   *Time to Complete:* 1 ELT period

Teaching Methods: Demonstration, laboratory exercise, and discussion

Materials: An ice cube; 1 teaspoon of salt; 1 piece of thread 8" long; 1 3"x4" index
   card; 1 marble; 2 craft sticks; 5 straight pins; 2 paper cups; 15 pennies; 1 3"x8"
   piece of paper; 1 ruler; 5" piece of masking tape; a small bag of popcorn; kernels
   of unpopped popcorn; 1 piece of string 12" long.

Objectives: The student will be able to demonstrate an understanding that a set of
   skills is necessary to solve problems in an orderly way; identify the sequential
   steps of the "scientific method"; state a hypothesis based on observation and
   prior knowledge, and prove a hypothesis by experimenting, revising and drawing conclusions; and, carry out the steps of the scientific method to solve a problem.

Procedure:	*Minutes:*
Introduce the activity by showing students these materials: 1 rubber band, 1 cotton ball, 1 plastic spoon, 1 ruler, and 1 5" piece of masking tape and then posing the question: "How can I make something out of these materials to shoot a cotton ball the farthest?"	15–20
Review the importance of using the "scientific method" as an orderly way to solve a scientific problem.	
From a deck of cards, give each student a card and have them find the other three people in the room with the same number to form their groups	
Each group will develop a hypothesis to solve the problem. Once the hypothesis is reviewed by the teacher, students will be given a set of materials, perform the task, revise it if necessary, redo the task, then draw a conclusion about what they have accomplished.	
A contest to determine which group can shoot the cotton ball the farthest will be held. Each group will then explain its hypothesis and conclusion.	
Groups will then rotate through four workstations, each with a problem to solve using the scientific method, and complete worksheets at each station. Students will be given 10 minutes at each workstation to complete their task.	45
Groups will hold "contests" for each completed task to determine which group had the most effective solution. Ideas will be exchanged and conclusions shared for each task.	15
Students will write in their science journals what they learned about the importance of using the scientific method to solve a problem and how it helped them solve the tasks in an orderly manner.	5

Evaluation: Each group will be evaluated in terms of a rubric designed
   to assess individual and group knowledge of the scientific method.

PHYSICAL EDUCATION AND HEALTH

Teacher: Nancy Angelini   *Course/Subject:* Health
Topic: Benefits of fitness   *Time to Complete:* 1 ELT period

Teaching Methods: Cooperative group learning, guided practice, and hands-on experience.

Materials: 6 magazine-size pictures related to fitness (e.g., weightlifter, individual shoveling snow, ballet dancer, printer, etc.), 6 manila envelopes, 6 pieces of white paper with graphic organizer design, and 6 plain white pieces of paper.

Objectives: Students will identify concepts related to fitness, list 10 benefits of a regular exercise regimen, and describe fitness principles that insure effective cardiovascular workouts.

Procedure:	*Minutes:*
As students enter the room, assign them a group number and instruct them to sit in the designated area. Instruct one student per group to read the envelop directions to their group.	5
Students engage in "Benefits of Fitness" puzzle activity. Cut each laminated picture into puzzlelike pieces, keeping each photograph separate. Insert the puzzle pieces for each picture into a separate manila envelop. Insert a plain white paper into each manila envelope, labeling it "graphic organizer."	15
Each group will review the ideas generated by other groups, write any notes that they feel are relevant to their topic, and refine their own organizer.	25
Each group will explain orally the relationship that their puzzle image has with the lesson and close the activity by saying, "You can't be the picture of health/fitness if you don't have all the pieces. Let's explore what fitness means to you and how it can benefit your body." Define physical fitness (i.e., the ability to carry out daily tasks without undue fatigue, enjoy leisure pursuits with energy, and the ability to meet the demands of unforeseen emergencies), question student's beliefs, and write out their lifestyle health choices. Working together, students must construct the puzzle, brainstorming as many connections as they can between the lesson and the puzzle image.	10
Brainstorm with the class how more activity can add to the daily routine to help improve fitness (followup to see if students incorporated the suggestions into their daily routines). Discuss with the class the importance of fitness and what can be done to improve it. Emphasize the principles of intensity, duration, and frequency.	10
Refer to activities brainstormed earlier. Discuss intensity, duration and frequency to activities students participate in daily.	10
Closure and homework assignment: Write an essay discussing the favorable conditions a fit person has over an unfit person on a day-to-day basis and provide specific examples to support the point of view.	10

Evaluation: Class participation and student essay.

PHYSICAL EDUCATION AND HEALTH

Teacher: Peter Filosa   *Course/Subject:* Health
Topic: Cardiopulmonary resuscitation   *Time to Complete:* 1 ELT period

Teaching Methods: Expository, audiovisual, demonstration, and Q&A

Materials: CPR videotapes, VCR and monitor, recitation model

Objectives: Students will demonstrate the techniques of administering CPR and an understanding of the basic anatomy and physiology of how CPR works.

Procedure:	*Minutes:*
Introduce CPR and its surrounding laws and liabilities (i.e., use of 911 and how to become CPR certified) and show a 5-minute CPR video clip.	20
Explain how an understanding of the human anatomy and physiology is necessary for administering CPR. Describe the effects of trauma on different systems of the body when CPR is administered. Cite the key facts and myths. Use a 7-minute CPR video clip.	20
Demonstrate proper techniques in the administration of CPR. Explain the effects of CPR in relationship to the expected outcome and what "first on scene" means. Emphasize pulse taking and proper timing. Divide into groups of two, and practice pulse taking.	35
Closure: Class discussion of the key points of CPR; have various students demonstrate the pulse check; respond to Q &A.	10

Evaluation: Written examination, an essay explaining the process, a demonstration of the process, and a case study analysis.

PHYSICAL EDUCATION AND HEALTH

Teacher: John Dagnese, Nick Zacchilli   *Course/Subject:* Physical Education

Topic: Weight lifting   *Time to Complete:* 1 ELT period

Teaching Methods: Demonstration, modeling, guided practice, hands-on experience, and partners.

Materials: Weight-training equipment, personal record sheets.

Objectives: The student will demonstrate the gain in weight lifting based on a pre-max test, a 70% of max routine for three classes, and a post-max assessment.

Procedure:	*Minutes:*
Introduce unit and explain objectives	5
Introduce equipment to be used and muscle areas being taxed during each group exercise. Demonstrate proper technique for each exercise.	15
Demonstrate the expected safety and spotting precautions to be used at all times at each exercise station. Stress the importance of safety and proper positioning of spotters.	10
Group prestretch led by instructor.	5
Each student will find the maximum amount of weight they can lift one time and record the weight on their personal record sheets.	30
When all the maximum amounts are recorded, the students will determine the 70% of their maximum and record same. The 70% weight will be the weight that is used for the next 3 classes and will be repeated in sets of 10–12 repetitions.	10
Poststretch exercises will be led by the instructor who will stress technique and concentration on appropriate muscles.	10

Evaluation: Written examination and performance assessment.

SUMMARY

As the lesson plans presented indicate, the central focus for the teaching and learning process in an ELT classroom shifts from the teacher to the student. Students are more actively engaged in the learning process and ultimately are more responsible for their own learning. The primary responsibility of the teacher is to identify the expected learning outcomes and to develop the classroom and outside activities that will allow students to attain the lesson objectives. With the time that the ELT period provides, teachers have a better opportunity to monitor individual student progress and to make individual adjustments or provide tutorials that will assist students in the learning process. Although some teachers feel that they are not "covering" as much of the curriculum content as they did in past years, they also state that entire concepts and ideas can be "uncovered" by students in a single ELT period. This was not the case in the past where the start-and-stop piecemeal approach to covering the curriculum dominated the teaching and learning process. Much of the fragmentation associated with traditional high school schedules can be eliminated with an ELT schedule.

Although the ELT schedule provides the organizational structure for the student-centered classroom, it is teachers who make it happen. The same veteran teachers who have been called upon to make some rather fundamental changes to teaching practices are the same individuals who are responsible for making the ELT schedule successful for their students. In the end, when students are successful, teachers are successful.

5

A GUIDE TO IMPLEMENTING EXTENDED LEARNING TIME

All men dream: but not equally.
Those who dream by night in the dusty recesses of their mind
Wake in the day to find that it was vanity:
But the dreamers of the day are dangerous men,
For they may act their dream with open eyes,
To make it possible.

T.E. Lawrence

Each school is unique in terms of its expectations, its curriculum, its culture, and many other aspects of the teaching and learning process. Therefore, each school should develop a plan of action that will meet the unique characteristics of that individual school and the expectations for student learning. With this in mind, the following reflective process was established to assist school personnel as a guide to focus on the many and varied aspects of schooling and the influences which interact to make a particular school the unique entity that it is.

It is important that each step in the resource guide be considered. Regardless of the mandate for change or the opposition to change that a school may experience, this resource guide can serve as the basis for successfully making the transition from a school with a traditional 6- or 7-period day schedule to a school with an ELT schedule. Of all the various efforts to restructure the American high school, the transformation from a teacher-centered industrial model to a student-centered ELT Model offers one of the most promising means of achieving this goal.

The 50 questions that follow, along with the models and checklists, were designed to avoid many of the problems that school personnel have faced when attempting to implement an ELT schedule.

155

IMPLEMENTATION CHECKLIST: PART I

Step 1: Consider what you want to do and why	
☐	1. What precisely are you trying to accomplish in your school in terms of the teaching and learning process?
☐	2. Why do you want to make the proposed changes? (Forcing you to answer these two questions helps avoid the common practice of moving directly to a canned solution; i.e., a solution in search of a problem or an opportunity.)

Step 2: Consider the Purpose, Future, and Vision of the School in relation to an ELT schedule.	
☐	3. What is the fundamental purpose of the school?
☐	4. What values, beliefs, and norms exist at the school?
☐	5. What changes in the culture of the school and the society it serves will have the greatest impact on the school's future?
☐	6. If the present course is maintained, what will the school look like in the future?
☐	7. What must the school do today and tomorrow to implement its vision for the future?

Step 3: Consider the Action Planning Team that will assist in implementing an ELT schedule.	
☐	8. How many people should be on the action planning team?
☐	9. What stakeholder groups should be represented on the team?
☐	10. How much authority will be vested, individually and collectively, in the team?
☐	11. What resources will be made available to the team?
☐	12. What personal characteristics will the team members bring to the team?

Step 4: Collect and analyze Awareness and Background Data that support the implementation of ELT.

☐	13. What data is available directly related to the problem or opportunity being considered?
☐	14. Does the data establish a discrepancy between what is and what should be?
☐	15. Is the discrepancy significant enough to warrant the intervention?
☐	16. Has the data been summarized in a way that can be understood by a variety of audiences?
☐	17. Does the data analysis serve as the basis for developing an action plan?

Step 5: Consider how the Rules, Roles, Relationships and Responsibilities will foster or constrain the implementation of ELT.

☐	18. What district policies, school polices, contractual agreements, etc., will foster or constrain the implementation of an ELT schedule?
☐	19. What roles exist within the district, school, etc., that will foster or constrain the implementation of an ELT schedule?
☐	20. What formal and information relationships exist within the district, the school, etc., that will foster or constrain the implementation of an ELT schedule?
☐	21. What bureaucratic, organizational, etc., responsibilities (i.e., authorizations) are required that will foster or constrain the implementation of an ELT schedule?

Step 6: Consider a variety of ELT Models before selecting the ELT schedule that will best foster student learning in your school.

The selection of a particular ELT Model will be a very important step in the process of moving from a traditional 6- or 7-period day to an ELT schedule. Although there are numerous ELT models (e.g., the AB or Alternating Day Model, the 4x4 or Semester Model, or the Trimester Model), there are also a number of variations to each model to accommodate local priorities, programs, staffing arrangements, and so forth. Rigid adherence to one particular model could result in opposition from key stakeholders or stakeholder groups within the school setting or within the school district. For example, there may be a great deal of concern for the performing arts if a semester or trimester model is adopted without provisions for the music program to meet throughout the year. Another concern among parents is the manner in which AP courses are dealt with. If a semester or trimester model is adopted, will the AP classes be scheduled during the fall semester or trimester? If the answer is yes, there will be a concern that students might not retain the factual information that they will need to take the AP exams that are scheduled in the spring. On the other hand, if the AP classes are scheduled in the spring, will students have sufficient time to "cover" the AP curriculum prior to the AP exams?

Similar questions might have to be considered with regard to technical and vocational programs, school-to-work programs, and so forth. If an AB Model is adopted, then the advantages of course sequence, the number of classes students and teachers have to prepare for will be a consideration during a semester. If a hybrid of one of the basic models is selected, then consideration has to be given to the nature of the model as it relates to the scheduling of individual student courses. Therefore, it is essential that the pros and cons for each model be carefully considered in terms of each individual school. The following, although it is not all inclusive, outlines a broad range of options that can be considered.

(Text continues on p. 166, after the model options.)

		A *Monday*	*B* *Tuesday*	*A* *Wednesday*	*B* *Thursday*	*A* *Friday*	*B* *Monday*
	Days						
P	*ELT 1*	1	2	1	2	1	2
E							
R	*ELT 2*	3	4	3	4	3	4
I							
O	*ELT 3*	5	6	5	6	5	6
D							

Alternate Day ELT Schedule—AB Model (6 Courses)

Six courses per year: 3 courses per day, all double periods *or* 1 ELT period. Each course meets on alternating days for the entire year.

		A *Monday*	*B* *Tuesday*	*A* *Wednes-* *day*	*B* *Thursday*	*A* *Friday*	*B* *Monday*
	Days						
P	*ELT 1*	1	2	1	2	1	2
E	*ELT 2*	3	4	3	4	3	4
R	*Single*	5	5	5	5	5	5
I							
O	*ELT 3*	7	6	7	6	7	6
D							

Alternate Day ELT Schedule—AB Model (7 Courses with 3 ELT periods and 1 Singleton daily)

Seven courses per year: 6 ELT periods and 1 short period. 4 courses per day: 3 ELT periods and 1 short period. Six long-block courses meet on alternating days for the entire year and 1 short period course meets daily for the entire year.

	Days	A Monday	B Tuesday	A Wednesday	B Thursday	A Friday	B Monday

Alternate Day ELT Schedule—AB Model (7 Courses with 2 ELT periods and 3 Singletons daily)

P E R I O D	Days	A Monday	B Tuesday	A Wednesday	B Thursday	A Friday	B Monday
	ELT 1	1	2	1	2	1	2
	Single	3	3	3	3	3	3
		4	4	4	4	4	4
		5	5	5	5	5	5
	ELT 2	7	6	7	6	7	6

Seven courses per year: 4 ELT periods and 3 short periods. Five courses per day: 2 ELT periods and 3 short periods. The short period courses meet daily for the entire year and the ELT period courses meet on alternating days for the entire year.

Alternate Day ELT Schedule—AB Model (8 Courses)

P E R I O D	Days	A Monday	B Tuesday	A Wednesday	B Thursday	A Friday	B Monday
	ELT 1	1	2	1	2	1	2
	ELT 2	3	4	3	4	3	4
	ELT 3	5	6	5	6	5	6
	ELT 4	7	8	7	8	7	8

Eight courses per year: 4 ELT period courses per day. Each course meets on alternating days for the entire year.

Quarter-On/Quarter-Off ELT Model (8 Courses)					
		Fall Semester		Spring Semester	
		Quarter 1	Quarter 2	Quarter 3	Quarter 4
P E R I O D	ELT 1	Course 1	Course 5	Course 1	Course 5
	ELT 2	Course 2	Course 6	Course 2	Course 6
	ELT 3	Course 3	Course 7	Course 3	Course 7
	ELT 4	Course 4	Course 8	Course 4	Course 8

Eight courses per year: All classes meet during ELT periods; 4 courses meet for ELT periods daily for the 1st and 3rd quarters and 4 courses meet for ELT periods daily for the 2nd and 4th quarters.

Basic 4/4 ELT Model (8 Courses)			
		Fall Semester	Spring Semester
P E R I O D	1	Course 1	Course 5
	2	Course 2	Course 6
	3	Course 3	Course 7
	4	Course 4	Course 8

Eight courses per year: 4 courses per day with 4 ELT periods. Each course meets every day for one semester per year.

4/4 ELT and AB ELT Model (8 Courses)				
		Fall Semester		*Spring Semester*
P E R I O D	*1*	Course 1		Course 6
	2	Course 2	Course 3	Course 2 | Course 3
	3	Course 4		Course 7
	4	Course 5		Course 8

This is essentially a combination of the 4x4 and the AB model. Some courses meet every day for an ELT period and some courses meet on alternate days for the entire year. The number of every day courses and alternate day courses can vary.

4/4 ELT, AB ELT and Short Period Model (15 Courses)				
		Fall Semester		*Spring Semester*
P E R I O D	*1*	Course 1		Course 9
	2	Course 2 | Course 3		Course 10 | Course 11
	3	Course 4 | Course 6		Course 4 | Course 6
		Course 5 | Course 7		Course 5 | Course 7
	4	Course 8		Course 12 | Course 13
				Course 14 | Course 15

This is a combination of all of the previous models. Some courses meet during an ELT period every day for one semester (Courses 1, 8, 9, and 12); some courses meet during an ELT period on alternate days for the entire year (Courses 2, 3, 10, and 11); some courses meet during short periods on alternate days for the entire year (Courses 4, 5, 6, and 7); and some courses meet for short periods on alternate days for a semester (Courses 12, 13, 14, and 15). This schedule offers the most options, but it is also the most complex.

Basic Trimester ELT Model (6 Courses)			
	Trimester 1 (60 Days)	*Trimester 2 (60 days)*	*Trimester 3 (60 days)*
Morning	Course 1	Course 3	Course 5
Lunch	Lunch		
Afternoon	Course 2	Course 4	Course 6

Six courses per year: 2 courses per trimester and all courses meet during ELT periods. Each course meets daily for 1 trimester.

Trimester ELT/Full-Year Singleton Model (7 Courses)			
	Trimester 1 (60 Days)	*Trimester 2 (60 days)*	*Trimester 3 (60 days)*
Trimester ELT	Course 1	Course 3	Course 5
Short Period	Course 7		
Trimester ELT	Course 2	Course 4	Course 6

Seven courses per year: 6 ELT period classes (Courses 1, 2, 3, 4, 5, and 6) and 1 short period classes (Course 7). Three courses per trimester and per day: 2 ELT period classes and 1 short period classes. The ELT period classes meet daily for 1 trimester and the short period classes meet daily for the entire year.

Trimester ELT/Full-Year Model (8 Courses)			
	Trimester 1 (60 Days)	*Trimester 2 (60 days)*	*Trimester 3 (60 days)*
Trimester ELT	Course 1	Course 3	Course 5
Short Period	Course 7		
Short Period	Course 8		
Trimester ELT	Course 2	Course 4	Course 6

Eight courses per year: 6 ELT period classes (Courses 1, 2, 3, 4, 5, and 6) and 2 short period classes (Courses 7 and 8). Four courses per trimester and per day: 2 ELT period classes and 2 short period classes. The ELT period classes meet daily for 1 trimester and the short period classes meet daily for the entire year.

Trimester ELT with Enhanced Learning Model (6 Courses)			
	Trimester 1 (60 Days)	*Trimester 2 (60 days)*	*Trimester 3 (60 days)*
Trimester ELT	Course 1	Course 3	Course 5
Trimester ELT	Course 2	Course 4	Course 6
Short Period	Course 1	Course 3	Course 5
Short Period	Course 2	Course 4	Course 6

Six courses per year: 2 courses per trimester with ELT and short periods. Each course meets twice daily: 1 ELT period and 1 short period per day for 1 trimester.

Core Program ELT/Term Model				
Morning Core Course (ELT Period)	English	Social Studies	Science	Mathematics
Year-Long Course (Short Period)	World Languages or Fine Arts			
Year-Long Course (Short Period)	World Languages or Fine Arts			
Afternoon Core Course (ELT Period)	English	Social Studies	Science	Mathematics

Eight courses per year: All English, Social Studies, Science and Mathematics classes meet during ELT periods. Four courses meet for ELT periods daily for the 1st and 3rd quarters and 4 courses meet for ELT periods daily for the 2nd and 4th quarters. World Language and Fine Arts classes meet for short periods for the entire year.

Customized ELT Model (Courses)							
Days		*Monday*	*Tuesday*	*Wednesday*	*Thursday*	*Friday*	*Monday*
P	ELT 1						
E							
R	ELT 2						
I							
O	ELT 3						
D							
	ELT 4						

Customize a model that may best meet the needs of a particular school in terms of the statement of purpose and expectations, curriculum, students, teachers, arrangements with other schools, businesses, etc.

SELECTING THE MODEL BEST FOR YOUR SCHOOL

When selecting the model for your school you need to match your expectations or the factors that are most important to you with the various models presented. Remember that you can always adapt a model to meet your own particular needs, but selecting the basic model can be difficult. Therefore, to assist you in this endeavor, utilize the following matrixes; place a plus (+), zero (0), or minus (-) in each box of the matrixes that appear on the next 3 pages.

(Text continues with Implementation Checklist: Part II on p. 170.)

STUDENT CONSIDERATIONS

Is this a schedule that offers:	"X" Periods/ day	AB Model	4x4 Model	60 60 60	75 75 30	75-15 75-15	Various Terms
Students an increased number of course choices?							
Students with an opportunity to earn an increased number of credits?							
Students extended learning time or for enrichment?							
Extended vocational and/or Tech Prep opportunities?							
Opportunities for students to repeat courses?							
Opportunities for students to accelerate the scope and sequence of courses?							
Reduced the number of classes students engage in per day/term?							

TEACHER CONSIDERATIONS

Is this a schedule that offers:	"X" Periods/ day	AB Model	4x4 Model	60 60 60	75 75 30	75-15 75-15	Various Terms
Teacher team planning time?							
Teacher Extended Learning Time for planning?							
Inexpensive implementation?							
Reduced teacher record-keeping?							
Reduced number of preparations assigned to teachers?							
Reduced the number of classes taught per day/term for teachers?							
Reduced student-teacher ratios on a daily basis?							
Reduced student-teacher ratios on a term/semester basis?							

LOGISTICAL CONSIDERATIONS

Is this a schedule that offers:	"X" Periods/ day	AB Model	4x4 Model	60 60 60	75 75 30	75-15 75-15	Various Terms
Inexpensive implementation?							
Reduced demands on a variety of resources?							
Flexibility?							
Adaptability?							
Easy implementation?							
Few political problems?							
Support for students?							
Possibilities for improved student discipline?							
Different formats to satisfy course needs or teacher preferences?							
Increased use of existing facilities?							
Increased use of community resources?							
Increased use of field trips?							
Decreased disruptions schoolwide?							
Decreased interruptions in instruction?							

IMPLEMENTATION CHECKLIST: PART II

Step 7: Review the Professional Literature and Research with regard to the ELT model you will adopt?	
☐	22. Have you identified the literature that supports the adoption of ELT?
☐	23. Have you identified the literature that opposes the adoption of ELT?

Step 8: Consider how the available resources will foster or constrain the implementation of ELT.	
☐	24. Have you identified the fiscal, human, and social capital necessary to implement the plan?
☐	25. Are the various resources you have identified realistic in terms of your plan and your school?
☐	26. What is the time line for implementing the plan?
☐	27. Will the various resources be available to you to implement your plan?

Step 9: Consider how your professional development plan will foster or constrain the implementation of ELT.	
☐	28. How much professional development time will be needed to prepare teachers for ELT?
☐	29. Who will provide the professional development activities (e.g., consultants, colleagues, graduate level courses, etc.)?
☐	30. What types of followup activities will be needed?
☐	31. What is the time line for implementing the plan?
☐	32. Will the various resources be available for the plan?

	Step 10: Consider how the Conditions for Change will foster or constrain the implementation of ELT.
☐	33. What is the prior history of successful change in the school setting?
☐	34. How dissatisfied are people with the current practices?
☐	35. Are or will the necessary resources to implement the daily instructional schedule available?
☐	36. How congruent is the proposed daily instructional schedule with existing and educationally sound practices?
☐	37. How many people will be affected by the ELT?
☐	38. How many of the key stakeholders and stakeholder groups are likely to support the new ELT?
☐	39. How many bureaucratic levels will be involved in implementing the new daily instructional schedule?
☐	40. How many units within the school will be affected by the change?
☐	41. How many people will be required to carry out the new schedule?
☐	42. How extensively has the new daily instructional schedule been communicated to the various stakeholder groups?

(Steps continue on next page.)

	Step 11: Consider how the Operational Methodology will foster or constrain the implementation of ELT.
☐	43. Did you describe the expected results from the change to the ELT?
☐	44. Have you established a timeline to measure key activities in your intervention?
☐	45. Have you established a chronological time frame for the development and implementation of the action plan?
☐	46. Have you established a means of monitoring the progress of the action plan?

	Step 12: Consider how you will Assess and Evaluate the impact of the ELT schedule.
☐	47. Have the quantitative results been analyzed?
☐	48. Have the quantitative results been disaggregated?
☐	49. Have the qualitative results been analyzed?
☐	50. Have the qualitative results been triangulated?

Assessing and evaluating the impact of the ELT schedule requires the collection of baseline data for the quantitative means of determining if the initiative is having the desired results. It should also be noted that not all aspects of the teaching and learning process can be readily assessed quantitatively. Therefore, both quantitative and qualitative means of assessing the impact of the ELT schedule on all aspects of the school should be employed. While data for most of the following indicators can be easily gathered, the impact on climate, on student-teacher relationships, on stress, on the quality and quantity of homework, on the variety of instructional strategies used throughout the school, and so forth are much more difficult to quantify. Using qualitative methods such as surveys, interviews, observations, and other qualitative processes can produce valid and valuable data with regard to the impact of the ELT schedule.

ASSESSMENT AND EVALUATION WORKSHEET

Indicators	Two Years Ago	Last Year	Present Year	Initial Year	2nd Year	3rd Year
Grades of "A"						
Grades of "B"						
Grades of "C"						
Grades of "D"						
Grades of "F"						
High Honor Roll						
Honor Roll						
Enrollment in AP Courses						
Enrollment in Honors Courses						
Enrollment in ( ) Courses						
Library/Media Center usage						
Disciplinary Referrals						
Suspensions: In-school						
Suspensions: Out-of-school						
Attendance: Students						
Tardiness: Students						
Attendance: Teachers						
Tardiness: Teachers						
Drop-Outs						
SAT Scores: Verbal						
SAT Scores: Math						
ACT Scores: Verbal						
ACT Scores: Math						

Indicators	Two Years Ago	Last Year	Present Year	Initial Year	2nd Year	3rd Year
AP English						
AP Social Studies						
AP Math						
AP Science						
AP World Language						
AP Other ( )						
PSAT Scores: Verbal						
PSAT Scores: Math						
State Testing: English						
State Testing: History						
State Testing: Math						
State Testing: Science						

SUMMARY

Most of the school improvement efforts to date have tended to focus on specific programs designed to improve the existing teaching and learning situations. However, those efforts have not yielded the consistency of results or the types of results that can be extended to other schools. But, the fundamental changes to the organizational structure of the school day that an Extended Learning Time schedule creates has generally produced consistent and predictable improvements to the cognitive, affective, and psychomotor aspects of a number of indicators of student learning, teaching strategies, school climate and culture. The positive assessment of the indicators listed previously has been documented in most schools that have adopted an ELT schedule, regardless of the ELT model that has been implemented.

As you proceed through the 12 steps of the process outlined in this chapter, be sure to answer each of the questions posed. If you have answered no to any of the questions, make certain that you have not overlooked an aspect or a consideration that will have a detrimental effect on the implementation of the ELT schedule. The use of the 50 questions, the checklists, and the qualitative assessment methods suggested should assist in your preliminary discussions, during the implementation of the ELT schedule, and as you review the impact the ELT schedule has had on your school at the end of each school year. If a well-developed plan is implemented with the support of key stakeholder groups and supported with adequate resources, then most of the outcomes are predictable. A review of those findings, both pro and con, will assist in the ongoing deliberations regarding the change to an ELT schedule.

6

EVALUATING THE QUANTITATIVE AND QUALITATIVE RESULTS OF EXTENDED LEARNING TIME

*To become aware of what is happening, I must pay attention with
an open mind. I must set aside my personal prejudices or bias.
Prejudiced people see only what fits those prejudices.*

Lao Tzu

Many new high school programs and organizational structures are planned and announced with high expectations, but are never evaluated in terms of their intended purpose or the expectations for them. This was not the case with ELT scheduling at MHS. There was a great deal of interest among the stakeholders about how well the ELT schedule was working. We regularly spoke with teachers and students to gather data regarding the ELT scheduling. Our action-planning team met weekly to review the various aspects of the ELT scheduling and to share our assessments, anecdotal comments, and direct classroom observations. What was the impact on the teaching and learning process as it related to the essential components of the adopted curriculum? Was the ELT schedule having the desired impact on student learning? What was the impact on teachers?

Because our primary purpose in adopting the 4x4 ELT model was to improve student learning, we needed to assess whether or not our primary goal was being achieved. However, student outcome measures, by themselves, would not tell the whole story. The quality of student learning is the product of the quality of the quality of services they receive. Thus, while looking at various indicators of student learning, there was also a need to focus on the nature and the quality of the intermediate steps related to student and faculty performance that lead to improved student learning. Therefore, both quantitative and qualitative data was gathered and analyzed to serve as the basis for both a formative and a summative evaluation of the ELT scheduling. Because a semester model had been adopted, quantitative data was available at the end of both the fall and spring semesters. Qualitative data, other than informal anecdotal comments from teachers and students, was not gathered until the end of the first full year of the ELT schedule. While there will be individuals who will want to rely solely on quantitative data, keep in mind that employing the triangulation of qualitative data can provide valuable information. Such a technique can provide valuable insights into the feelings of the various stakeholder groups and at the same time provide insights into the feelings of individuals that provide plausible explanations for similar observations.

STUDENT LEARNING

Attempts to improve student learning were not limited to just adding classes to the students' schedules, but to broadening student learning in all of the core disciplines. At the same time, students were given the opportunity to engage in an expanded elective program that would enrich their learning in a variety of disciplines, including the practical and fine arts, physical education, and health.

The first indicator of the impact of the ELT schedule on students was that students were selecting the equivalent of eight classes per year, with no study hall classes. However, the organizational delivery system that allowed them to enroll in more classes during the course of a year also allowed them to prepare for fewer classes during the course of a given day. Because the graduation requirements had been increased, students were selecting more classes in the core disciplines of English language arts, history and social sciences, mathematics, science and technology, and world languages. Not only were students engaged in more classes, there was an impact on the nature of the courses that they were taking. With the reality that they would only have to prepare for four classes per day, the percentage of students selecting the more challenging Advanced Placement (AP; 130-level) and honors level (120-level) classes rose, with a corresponding decrease in the number of students enrolled in the normal college preparatory (110-level) classes. Figure 6.1 illustrates this dramatic shift in the course selection practices by students preparing for the ELT schedule.

FIGURE 6.1. STUDENT COURSE SELECTION BY
COURSE LEVEL IN CORE DISCIPLINES

Course Level	1995-96	1996-97	Average	1997-98	+/-
130	2.5%	2.9%	2.7%	3.3%	+0.6%
120	43.3%	43.0%	43.2%	52.6%	+9.4%
110	54.2%	54.1%	54.1%	44.1%	-10.0%

Not only did students elect higher level classes, but their achievement at the end of both the fall and spring semester was better, as was indicated by their attaining higher grades in their classes. Figure 6.2 illustrates that while more students were enrolled in honors-level classes, the percentage of students attaining As increased while the percentage of students earning Bs and Cs decreased slightly. However, there was an unexpected downside in student achievement: There was an increase in the number of students who received failing grades. An analysis of the grades indicated that two factors were primarily responsible for the increase in failures. First, prior to implementing the ELT schedule there was a great deal of concern regarding the impact that student absenteeism would have on student achievement. As a result, a strict attendance policy was adopted with the intent of reducing student absenteeism. Figure 6.3 indicates that student attendance did improve. Whether it was the direct result of the new attendance policy or the feeling frequently expressed by students that they "couldn't afford to miss class" was not determined. However, upon checking student failures, it was discovered that approximately 60–70 percent of the students who received failing grades did so because of the attendance policy and not because they were unable to comprehend the essential learnings and learn the basic skills of the course.

A second factor influencing the rise in students receiving failing grades was the performance of the freshman class. The number of students who earned failing grades was more than double the failure rate of previous classes. The obvious question was: "Is the failure rate the result of the ELT schedule coupled with the transition from a middle school to the high school." A review of the academic grades of the members of the freshman class, in prior years, indicated that the members of the class had a higher failure rate at previous grade levels. A further analysis indicated that the

FIGURE 6.2. STUDENT GRADES IN CORE DISCIPLINES

Course Level	1995-96	1996-97	Average	1997-98	+/-
A	22.9%	30.8%	28.0%	31.5%	+3.5%
B	40.5%	36.9%	38.3%	34.2%	-1.6%
C	21.1%	20.7%	20.9%	18.2%	-0.9%
D	9.7%	8.2%	8.8%	9.3%	+0.8%
F	5.8%	2.8%	4.0%	6.6%	+2.6%

aggregate grades of the freshman classes were higher at the high school level than they had been in previous years. This was also supported by the overwhelming endorsement of members of the freshman class for the ELT schedule in the survey conducted at the close of the school year.

Figure 6.3 indicates that the average daily attendance during the initial year of ELT scheduling improved slightly when compared with the 1995-96 and the 1996-97 school years. Whether this increase was the result of a more restrictive attendance policy or the result of more positive student-teacher interactions was difficult to determine. Nonetheless, the increases in student attendance and student grades were positive findings.

FIGURE 6.3. STUDENT ATTENDANCE

Attendance	1995-96	1996-97	Average	1997-98	+/-
Totals	91.6%	91.7%	91.6%	92.1%	+0.5%

On the more positive side, the criteria for attaining both high honors and honors was also raised for the 1997-98 school year. However, as Figure 6.4 indicates, the percentages of students attaining honor-roll status increased substantially under the ELT plan. Although these indicators over the course of a full-year illustrate a positive impact of the ELT on student learning, they also indicate the impact that the ELT schedule had on student achievement.

The percentage of students planning on attending colleges and universities, the admissions rates, and the prestige of the colleges and universities

FIGURE 6.4. STUDENT HONOR ROLL

Honor Roll	1995-96	1996-97	Average	1997-98	+/-
High Honors	10.4%	13.8%	12.0%	16.9%	+4.9%
Honors	15.1%	15.6%	15.3%	19.4%	+4.1%
Totals	25.5%	29.4%	27.3%	36.3%	+9.0%

that accepted MHS students was not negatively impacted by the ELT schedule. In fact, the number of students who planned to attend and who were accepted to four-year colleges and universities continued to grow. Over the years, this rate had continually risen from 60% of the graduating class to the present rate of approximately 80%. The fact that MHS students were accepted to as many, if not more, of the more prestigious colleges and universities than with the traditional seven-period day schedule quelled much of the speculation that college admissions officers would not look favorably upon applicants from a school that had implemented an ELT schedule.

With regard to the college preparatory students, one of the key questions that all of the key stakeholder groups asked was, "What impact will the ELT schedule have on SAT scores?" Although it was suggested that the impact on SAT scores would be minimal during the initial year of the ELT schedule, there was still a great deal of concern regarding the scores. The scores, outlined in Figure 6.5, indicated that students at MHS scored at approximately the same level that they had during the previous year and that the percentage of students taking the SATs was approximately the same as in previous years.

Of more significance were the scores attained on the Advanced Placement (AP) tests. Modifications were made to accommodate students who enrolled in AP classes. Essentially, the amount of actual time allotted for AP classes was increased by 40%. This accommodation, which provided students with an ELT period each day during the fall semester and an ELT period–alternate-day schedule during the spring semester, was made to allow senior students to earn grades in their AP classes that would appear on transcripts, while keeping them engaged longer for the AP exams administered during the spring semester. The results indicate that a greater number of students earned scores of 5 and 4 than in previous years. However, it should also be noted that a combination of the increasing cost of taking the AP

FIGURE 6.5. SCHOLASTIC ASSESSMENT TESTS (SAT)

SATs	Score	1995-96	1996-97	Average	1997-98	+/-
Mathematics	National	508	511	----	512	*+1*
	State	504	508	----	508	*0*
	MHS	486	505	*496*	500	*+4*
	% of Class	80.0%	78.0%	*79.0%*	80.0%	*+1.0%*
Verbal	National	505	505	---	505	*0*
	State	507	508	---	508	*0*
	MHS	494	505	*500*	506	*+6*
	% of Class	80.0%	78.0%	*79.0%*	80.0%	*+1.0%*

exams and the decrease in the number of colleges and universities that are willing to accept the results of AP for credit has resulted in a decrease in the number of students who take these tests. Figure 6.6 indicates the change in the percentages of students earning grades of 5 and 4 on the AP tests.

FIGURE 6.6. ADVANCED PLACEMENT (AP) TESTS

AP Tests	Score	1995-96	1996-97	Average	1997-98	+/-
AP Testing Totals	5	8.9%	8.7%	*8.8%*	9.9%	*+1.1%*
	4	26.6%	20.3%	*23.2%*	33.3%	*+10.1%*
	3	34.2%	37.7%	*35.9%*	33.3%	*-2.5%*
	2	22.8%	27.5%	*25.1%*	19.8%	*-5.3%*
	1	7.6%	5.8%	*7.0%*	3.7%	*-3.3%*

The overall impact of the ELT schedule on student learning appeared to be positive. Students were engaging in a greater number of courses, were selecting higher level courses, and were achieving higher grades in their core courses. While it will be a few years before trends can be established in norm-referenced tests, preliminary indicators tend to support the hypothesis that such scores will increase.

Although the comments of students regarding the 4x4 ELT schedule ranged from "I hate it" to "I love it," most of the comments were positive. Some student comments were:

- "The classes are longer, but more interesting. It's a lot less stressful than previous years. We do a lot more labs this year and that is also better."

- "The classes go by quick and you don't have to cram all your work into a short period."

- "I like being able to ask questions and have the teachers go into detail because we have time to review."

- "It makes the day seem shorter. Teachers are also able to use different and exciting methods to get the key concepts across to their students."

- "Each period has one hour more time so you can ask more questions and finish more of the class work."

- "There is more time to study for classes. You learn more with longer periods and there is more time to work with others in group activities."

- "There is more time for teachers to explain the material and more time to ask questions to gain a better understanding of the material. I am also less stressed because I only have to worry about four classes instead of seven classes."

- "The thing that I like the most is the fact that we are gaining more knowledge. I am also able to complete my homework more completely."

The comments made by teachers with regard to student learning were similar to those expressed by students. The following are just a few of the teacher comments regarding the impact that the ELT schedule had on student learning:

- "There is more time to have students practice concepts."
- "Students can do more in-depth work in each class."

- "It provides more flexibility in terms of meeting with students. It increases opportunities to develop new ways of providing information in more stimulating ways."

- "Students have time to 'think.' You can have uninterrupted class discussions and it is a much better arrangement for small group activities that then lead to presentations to the whole group."

- "I don't have to repeat myself 10 times in 2 days. Also, I feel I am able to help the student who has learning difficulties. I have more time to get to know students' abilities and personalities."

- I have a chance to answer questions and tie loose ends to a topic before students are sent home to practice."

- "The students have fewer classes to focus on and I have more time in class for them to be the center of the learning process."

- "Students getting involved in the learning process through more activities in class. There is a greater flexibility for me to select certain themes to explore in depth. I am probably getting to know the kids better and varying the instruction. It's really got a lot of good points and I may be forgetting a few!"

- "There is time to cover concepts in more depth without interruption."

- "There is more time to help individual students. There is also more time to do different types of assignments."

CURRICULUM

At the onset of the discussions regarding the implementation of the ELT schedule, two curricular goals were established: to keep the best of the past and present, while moving MHS toward a new vision of academic achievement for all students, and to expand the graduation requirements for all students in the core academic disciplines while maintaining our rich elective offerings. One of the initial results of the implementation of an ELT schedule was the adoption of increased graduation requirements. Students are now required to successfully complete the equivalent of four years of courses or four credits in the core disciplines. This doubled the requirements in history and social science, mathematics, and science and technology. In addition, all students are also required to successfully complete three years or three credits in a world language other than English, one credit in the fine arts, and to demonstrate proficiency in the use of computer technology. As the enrollments in Figure 6.7 indicate, all disciplines have benefited from the implementation of the ELT schedule. Of even more significance was the that an increasing number of students were enrolling in more than one course per year in each of the core disciplines. This phenomenon led to a re-examination of the scope and sequence of courses in the core curriculum in each discipline, of the essential learnings for each discipline, and of the grade-level expectations for each discipline.

FIGURE 6.7. CLASS SIZE BY DISCIPLINE

Discipline	1995-96			1996-97			1997-98		
	# Sec	# Stu FTE	Class Size	# Sec	# Stu FTE	Class Size	# Sec	# Stu FTE	Class Size
English Lang. Arts	54.0	1011	18.7	49.0	1031	21.0	62.0	1129	18.2
History Social Sci.	51.0	1135	22.3	54.0	1288	23.4	70.0	1421	20.3
Mathematics	56.0	1034	18.9	58.0	1269	21.5	86.0	1539	17.9
Science & Tech	46.0	886	19.3	49.0	1036	20.7	70.0	1386	19.8
World Languages	36.0	630	18.0	40.0	814	19.9	46.0	773	16.8
Business Education	11.0	102	9.3	15.0	370	24.7	22.0	381	17.3
Family & Cons. Sci.	8.0	73	9.1	10.0	165	16.5	10.0	149	14.9
Trade & Industry	15.0	144	9.6	15.0	188	12.5	16.0	183	11.4
Video/Program	3.0	72	24.0	3.0	75	25.0	3.0	63	21.0
Music	2.5	167	55.7	5.0	266	44.5	6.0	243	39.0
Visual Arts	5.0	80	16.0	11.0	283	25.7	15.0	329	21.9
P.E./Health	27.0	683	24.9	27.0	658	24.4	40.0	820	20.5
Totals	314.5	6017	19.1	336.0	7443	22.2	446.0	9407	18.9

Teachers are asking difficult questions concerning the curriculum content for each course as they map the course syllabi, the pacing guides, the activities that students will engage in, and the means of assessing student progress. The entire process of curriculum revision and renewal has become an ongoing reality. It is not an esoteric exercise to teachers, it is the reality of what they are doing on a day-to-day basis. The efforts of teachers to align the state-mandated curriculum frameworks with the locally adopted curriculum and the curriculum that is taught in classrooms daily has became a reality.

Students sensed a change in the manner in which the curriculum was presented in class. Statements such as these were echoed by a number of students:

- "I like the fact that we get more done and we have time to have group discussions which help me learn. I also like the fact that the day goes by quicker."

- "I like the fact that I only have to study for four tests instead of seven. I also like having less homework."

- "Although you usually get more assignments per night, it is for fewer classes which allows you to prepare better. It allows you to prepare better for tests. The homework is based on the same work so it is easier, even though it takes longer to complete."

- "You can have things explained better in the four-period day. You can go into depth in a subject. There is more time to explain and more time to do work."

- "There is more time to learn the lessons better and you don't have such a variety of homework each night."

- "There is more time to explain things in class. It seems more enjoyable and there is not as much homework. This allows you to do better work with less stress relative to studying for class."

- "The teachers go over the information in more detail and I seem to keep more knowledge about things. I think that teachers take more time to explain things as well because they know they have more time. Everything does not seem as rushed. It was awesome!!"

- "More gets done. Instead of taking a week to go through a chapter it takes half the time. There is more time to get involved in class. There is more time at the end of class to start on homework so if you have any questions you can ask them. You can also take your time on tests."

Just as the students sensed a difference in the classroom in terms of the curriculum and with regard to homework, so did the teachers who tended to offer similar comments. These teacher comments illustrate the congruence between the perceptions of students and teachers with regard to the curriculum:

+ "I like not rushing through homework review and still having plenty of time for the day's lesson."

+ "I like being able to complete a whole unit in one day thoroughly."

+ "I am more relaxed during each ELT class because I do not feel rushed to go over homework. I can model or have students discover new concepts. I have time for practice, check for understanding and send students home confident they have a good change of being successful on homework!"

+ "I can spend more time on the main ingredients of my curriculum."

+ "I can concentrate on the bigger picture of the course. Students have less distractions."

+ "The four-period day allows for continuity in teaching time, more flexibility, and less fragmentation."

+ "The ELT has allowed me to go into greater detail on critical thinking issues than I have in the past."

+ "I like the longer preparation time and the extra time in class to complete work. I like the time available to complete more hands-on lab work. I also like the extra time—I need it—for AP classes."

+ "The four-period day allows or requires different teaching. It is not 'covering' material but the instruction and learning of skills and material."

+ "Teaching three classes is less fragmented."

TEACHERS

In addition to their curriculum work, teachers have benefited from not only a reduction in class size, but from the total number of students they meet daily. As Figure 6.7 (p. 185) indicates, the average teacher meets with between 60–75 students per day as opposed to 100–125 students per day with a 7-period day. Nonetheless, most teachers indicate that they are working much harder now than they have in the past. They felt that they were spending much more time preparing for class and correcting student homework and papers. The amount of time spent preparing for class was really not surprising considering that teachers recognized the need for increasing the variety of instructional strategies they were using in any given class period coupled with a different perspective of the curriculum content. Even though some teachers had more difficulty than others, most teachers agreed that the essential knowledge and skills for each course could be effectively taught in a 4x4 ELT schedule.

Overall, there was a general consensus that students are more engaged in their work in school, although there was some question regarding the "coverage" of content, the "depth" of student learning, and retention of student learning. However, as one teacher put it, "In the past I would 'cover' 300 pages of material and the students would remember 100 pages. Now I 'cover' 200 pages of material and the students remember the material from 150 pages. Which would you rather have?"

Although the coverage question will take time to overcome, teachers did overwhelmingly cite a number of indicators that students were achieving more academically and were more engaged than in past years. The following statements about students in the ELT schedule were endorsed by more than 75% of the faculty:

- Students were mastering the important concepts and skills in their respective classes;
- Students are thinking more analytically and critically in class this year than in past years;
- There is a greater focus on active student interaction during class time this year;
- Student attendance in classes is better; and
- Students were achieving better in an ELT classroom than in a classroom with only a 45 to 55-minute period.

On a more subtle note, teachers indicated that they were spending more time collaborating with colleagues than ever before, were better able to personalize instruction during class time to meet the individual needs of students, had greater flexibility in choosing from a variety of instructional strategies, and were lecturing far less than in previous years. Teachers did indicate that the comprehensive professional development program that they had an opportunity to participate in concurrently and prior to the implementation of the ELT schedule had helped them to develop new and exciting instructional strategies, had helped them to improve their overall teaching performance, and had helped them to achieve their personal and professional goals relative to MHS.

Similar results were reported by students, who also felt that they were more engaged with fellow students, that teachers were spending more time in class with them personally, and that they were engaging in a wider variety of classroom activities. Ironically, they also indicated that teachers were spending too much time lecturing. Perhaps the transformation from a primarily teacher-centered classroom to a more student-centered classroom gave both teachers and students an opportunity to reflect upon their past experiences from a new perspective.

These teacher comments are illustrative of the impact that the ELT schedule has had on their preparation and teaching strategies:

- "Being responsible for the preparation and delivery in three classes has resulted in my being more effective overall."

- "I like being able to work more with a fewer number of students at one time. I enjoy using a variety of teaching methods and the students like this also."

- "I like having the preparation period provided in the four-period day. It allows me to assess how well students have understood concepts so that I can make plans while in school that are contingent upon that assessment."

- "I like the longer classes which allow me to be more creative in the class. I like teaching only three classes per semester."

- "It provides quality time to prepare quality lessons as well as time to teach the lesson. There is sufficient time for monitoring student progress and adjusting to their needs and this does improve performance."

- "I like the longer prep period, the fewer classes and the challenge to 'stretch' professionally."

SCHOOL CLIMATE

The establishment of more student-centered classrooms was certainly a goal of the 4x4 ELT schedule. There was also a hope that the new schedule would provide a means of moving the school from one based on the industrial assembly-line model to one that would prepare all students to meet the highly skilled needs of the twenty-first century. If successful, both of these factors would impact the school climate.

Although both teachers and students reported no a significant difference in the school climate, a difference was noticeable in terms of student behavior. Both teachers and students indicated that the day seemed to go by much more quickly than in previous years. While teachers felt a little more stressed because of the amount of time they were spending preparing for class, correcting papers, and redefining the essentials of their curriculum, students indicated that they were far less stressed by the demands of their courses and the amount of homework that they were required to do each evening. Although there was more homework per class, students noted that fewer classes more than compensated for the increase in the amount of homework per class.

Another very noticeable difference was observable in the physical configuration of the classrooms. Rows of seats facing the teacher, previously the norm, were replaced by other arrangements (e.g., horseshoe arrangements, clusters of desks facing one another, ovals, and others). The arrangements implied that students were expected to contribute to the teaching and learning process in those classrooms. They were expected to assume a greater responsibility for their own learning and would be held accountable.

Overall, the climate appeared more peaceful and, as one person noted, "more civilized." With fewer passing times between classes per day, the school seemed much quieter and less hurried. Another indicator occurred on early release days. On those days, each class was shortened to approximately 45-minutes. Both students and teachers indicated that they felt very rushed. As one teacher noted, "I don't know how I ever got anything done in a 45-minute period. Those poor kids!" These sentiments are summed in these teacher comments:

- ◆ "The four-period day allows the teacher to concentrate on a more focused body of material. It reduces some of the stress of constant motion and allows teachers to take a breather."

- ◆ "The four-period day gives me more time to spend with fewer classes. The day goes by faster."

- ◆ "I do not have to rush through a lesson and there is time to vary activities. The rotating schedule is great."

♦ "There is less disruption due to the constant moving of students from one place to another. Thus, there is less wasting of time and better classes."

Not only did teachers recognize that the pace was not as frantic with the ELT schedule, students also commented on the relative calm of the day in the ELT schedule:

♦ "The classes are longer, but more interesting. It's a lot less stressful than previous years. We do a lot more labs this year and that is also better."

♦ "I like only having four classes per day because it is less stressful. Teachers explain things more in depth because they have more time."

♦ "The things I like most is that teachers aren't frantic and rushing to get things done in the 83-minute classes as they were in the 45-minute classes."

♦ "I like the fact that we don't have to get stressed out over seven classes all year long. It is also good that the teachers give us more time in class to ask questions and to get more information on confusing points in my classes."

While the climate appeared much calmer, there were still isolated incidents and the cumulative behaviors of students that resulted in student suspensions. While Figure 6.8 indicates that the percentages of students suspended declined only slightly, a review of the suspension data reveals that most incidents involving a disruption to the school environment were not the direct result of disruptive behavior or confrontation behavior on the part of students and teachers. More than 50% of all suspensions were the direct result of students "cutting" or "skipping" class or school and then not assuming the responsibility for their actions.

FIGURE 6.8. STUDENT SUSPENSIONS

Suspensions	1995-96	1996-97	Average	1997-98	+/-
Totals	13.9%	11.5%	12.7%	11.3%	-1.4%

One of the direct benefits of the ELT schedule was the ability to analyze the data collected to determine the effect of the ELT schedule on all aspects of the school. Although schools collect and have available a great deal of data, this data frequently does not produce any real information that is useful for improving the school. Knowing that the results of the ELT scheduling would be scrutinized, all data was disaggregated and reviewed in terms of subsets and individual factors that ultimately produced summative data. Just as the results of the SAT data provided information that was beneficial in establishing the need for greater student enrollment in the core disciplines, disaggregated data regarding students who were suspended provided better insights into those students. A closer look at the individual characteristics of students suspended indicated that:

- 4 of 5 students who were suspended came from families with special circumstances (single parent families, divorced parents, and others);

- 1 of 2 students who were suspended was involved with the court system;

- 1 of 3 students who were suspended was a special needs student;

- 1 of 5 students who were suspended became a dropout;

- 1 of 10 students who were suspended were in a foster care situation; and

- 1 of 20 students who were suspended from school was a student who had previously dropped out of school and returned.

While some of the students fit into more than one of the categories listed, only 1 of 10 students who were suspended did not fit into any of the categories noted above. From a more positive perspective, the number of students who had previously dropped out of school and successfully returned to school increased. This need to disaggregate data to develop useful information served as the impetus for the administration and faculty at MHS to reassess the disciplinary procedures and practices for all students. The result was the development of a new set of consequences that placed more of a premium on the active involvement of the student in the decision making process.

Furthermore, although the percentage of students who were suspended constituted only a small segment of the MHS student population, the suspended students could not be simply dismissed as "those students." Rather, the individual students who fell into that category tended to be the "at-risk" students who required a good deal of attention and services from a variety of professionals. Because our goal is to educate all students, our success in terms of academic achievement with all segments of the student population (the highly motivated, high achieving student; the average student; and the at-risk student) will, to a large degree, determine the overall effectiveness of MHS.

EXTERNAL FACTORS

Although the primary reasons for moving to an ELT schedule were based upon the curriculum and student learning, there were external factors that needed to be addressed. For example, there was the realization that MHS would have to meet the requirements established by the state mandates and to address the recommendations of the regional accrediting agency, the NEASC. The implementation of the 4x4 ELT schedule allowed MHS to meet all of the specific mandates established by the Massachusetts Department of Education in compliance with the Education Reform Act of 1993. Furthermore, the report of our efforts from a curriculum and instruction perspective, from a programmatic and personnel perspective, and from a physical and fiscal perspective allowed MHS to earn full and continuing accreditation from the NEASC.

Locally, the ELT schedule allowed MHS to eliminate all study halls and still be fiscally responsible to the community. Through the efforts of the central administration, the school committee, and the community, adequate resources to hire additional personnel as well as the textbooks, supplies, materials, and equipment needed to fully implement the 4x4 ELT schedule were made available to each class.

SUMMARY

In evaluating the overall success of the 4x4 ELT schedule at MHS, we looked at each of our goals and collected both quantitative and qualitative data. This data was analyzed from different perspectives, and where necessary modifications were made to the program. It is important to stress that the disaggregation of quantitative data and the triangulation of qualitative data provided the planning team with credible information regarding the implementation of the 4x4 ELT model at MHS. Furthermore, by engaging all of the various stakeholders in the process of transforming a traditional high school into a more student-centered high school, from the very beginning, was positive. The input from these stakeholder groups, whether in the form of suggestions or merely posing questions, was certainly a valuable asset as we moved through the process. Although there is still much work to be done to refine the curriculum and the teaching process, to refine and develop new strategies and policies for the ELT classroom, the barrage of questions and negative comments have definitely subsided. The question now focuses on how the process can be improved. By the end of the first full year of the 4x4 ELT schedule at MHS, most of the critics became silent when confronted with both the quantitative and the qualitative results of the ELT schedule.

Finally, when specifically asked what recommendations they would make to improve the ELT schedule, students responded:

- "I don't have any."
- "I'd recommend this schedule to other schools."
- "I think this system is fine and is working out pretty well."
- "Vary class activities."
- "Have more projects and less homework. Utilize less lecturing to help people understand the concepts."
- "Teachers need to give less emphasis to the content so they can concentrate more on teaching. Teach more about less, rather than less about more. If we weren't so rushed, we could understand things a lot better."

While there is always room for improvement, one final question was posed to both students and teachers at the close of the initial year of the 4x4 ELT schedule. Would you prefer the 4x4 ELT schedule or a return to the 7-period day. The responses were overwhelming. Approximately 80 percent of the student body and slightly more than 70 percent of the faculty indicated that they would not want to return to the "old" 7-period day. As one faculty member put it, "You would have to drag me screeching and clawing all the way back to a seven-period day. I just don't think I could go through that again!"

APPENDIX

MILFORD HIGH SCHOOL STATEMENT OF PURPOSE

The mission of Milford High School is to provide an educational process in a safe school environment that will foster critical thinking and the acquisition of knowledge and skills; a self-discipline that will encourage academic excellence, self-sufficiency and personal responsibility; and, a respect for diversity, all of which will prepare students for life-long learning, a high standard of ethics and a willingness to make a positive contribution to society.

STUDENT EXPECTATIONS

Academic Excellence—Students will:

- ◆ Practice creative and critical thinking;
- ◆ Collect, organize, interpret and evaluate information to arrive at informed conclusions;
- ◆ Strive to become objective listeners;
- ◆ Learn to recognize and value innovative ideas;
- ◆ Communicate ideas effectively in various modes (verbal, non-verbal, written, etc.);
- ◆ Employ problem-solving and decision-making techniques;
- ◆ Strive to achieve accuracy, precision, and clarity;
- ◆ Meet the highest scholastic expectations that each is capable of attaining;
- ◆ Develop an awareness of the arts; and
- ◆ Demonstrate sufficient mastery of technology and its application to the education, work, and global environments.

Personal Responsibility and Self-Esteem—Students will:

♦ Foster an educational environment that is free from all bias;

♦ Assume responsibility for their own academic growth;

♦ Actively participate in the learning process;

♦ Realistically assess themselves—their talents, personal worth, and areas of needed improvement;

♦ Apply honesty, integrity, and fairness when dealing with themselves and others;

♦ Practice and advocate positive social behavior; and

♦ Take personal responsibility for the impact of their words and actions on themselves and others.

Social Expectations—Students will:

♦ Learn to understand, appreciate, and respect individual differences;

♦ Develop an understanding of and a respect for different cultures, religions, and traditions;

♦ Acquire an awareness and understanding of various cultures and their unique contributions to science, mathematics, technology, literature, and the arts;

♦ Demonstrate the ability to work harmoniously and effectively outside the traditions of their own cultural mores;

♦ Be informed regarding environmental and civic issues;

♦ Become personally involved in community service;

♦ Actively participate in the democratic process;

♦ Assume responsibility in dealing with health and environmental issues, and recognize the rights and responsibilities of individuals in these matters.

SCHOOL EXPECTATIONS

Academic Excellence—Milford High School will:

♦ Support, expand, and evaluate a curriculum that provides opportunities for the student to continue to develop and maintain mental, emotional, and physical health;

♦ Assist the student in acquiring the necessary skills to read intelligently, to think logically, and to communicate effectively;

♦ Provide and encourage opportunities for professional development;

♦ Provide students with the opportunity to achieve their highest expectations for individual improvement; and

♦ Provide the technological environment for learning to live in a rapidly changing electronic age.

Personal Responsibility and Self-Esteem—Milford High School will:

♦ Promote cocurricular activities and encourage increased student participation to help form positive self-images and define personal goals;

♦ Promote a safe school environment that is free from drugs and violence;

♦ Provide a framework that will encourage greater parental responsibility and participation in the educational process; and

♦ Provide a framework that will require that students be actively involved in and accountable for their learning.

Respect for Diversity—Milford High School will:

♦ Design and implement a variety of learning experiences that enable the student to function in a diverse society;

♦ Foster an educational environment that is free from all bias; and

♦ Advocate the philosophy that diversity enriches both the individual and society.

Positive Contribution to Society—Milford High School will:

- ◆ Coordinate all components to aid the student in becoming a productive citizen of the school and the community;

- ◆ Foster the cooperative effort of the administration, faculty, parents, and community in emphasizing excellence and the personal and social development of the student;

- ◆ Continue to endorse and support the concept that the school is a community resource center that fosters life-long learning;

- ◆ Encourage greater involvement of private industry and members of the community in sharing their expertise and the school and in enhancing opportunities for the students; and

- ◆ Further develop a cooperative program with business/industrial management to provide financial assistance and technological support to our educational system.

REFERENCES

Achilles, C. M., Reynolds, J. S., & Achilles, S. H. (1999). *Problem analysis: Responding to school complexity.* Larchmont, NY: Eye On Education.

Aguilera, R. V. (1996). Block scheduling: Changing the system. *Curriculum Report, 25*(5), 1–4.

Alam, D., & Seick, R. E., Jr. (1994). A block schedule with a twist. *Phi Delta Kappan, 75*(2), 732–733.

Anderson, L. W., & Walberg, H. J. (1994). *Time piece: Extending and enhancing learning time.* Reston, VA: National Association of Secondary School Principals.

Anderson, R., Brozynski, D. & Lett, D. (1996). Scheduling with purpose: Key people and key objectives. *High School Magazine, 3*(3), 24–26.

Armstrong, T. (1994). *Multiple intelligences in the classroom.* Alexandria, VA: Association for Supervision and Curriculum Development.

Bateson, D. J. (1990). Science achievement in semester and all-year courses. *Journal of Research in Science Teaching, 27*(1), 233–240.

Barth, R. S. (1988). Principals, teachings, and school leadership. *Phi Delta Kappan, 69*(4), 682–686.

Beane, J. A. (1992). Crating an integrative curriculum: Making the connections. *NASSP Bulletin, 76*(547), 46–54.

Berkbuegler, R., & Webb, L. D. (1998). *Personal learning plans for educators.* Reston, VA: National Association of Secondary School Principals.

Bernhardt, V. L. (1998). *Data analysis for comprehensive schoolwide improvement.* Larchmont, NY: Eye on Education, Inc.

Black, S. (1998). Learning on the block. *American School Board Journal, 185*(1), 32–34.

Blaz, D. (1998). *Teaching foreign language in the block.* Larchmont, NY: Eye on Education.

Bloom, B. (Ed.) (1956). *Taxonomy of educational objectives.* New York: Longman.

Brown, E. D. (1996). We "tri-ed" the alternative: Trimester scheduling worked for us. *High School Magazine, 3*(3), 34–39.

Bruckner, M. (1997). Eavesdropping on change: Listening to teachers during the first year of an extended block schedule. *NASSP Bulletin, 81*(593), 42–52.

Bruner, J. (1966). *Toward a theory of instruction.* Cambridge, MA: Harvard University Press.

Buckman, D. C., King, B. B., & Ryan, S. (1994). Block scheduling: A means to improve school climate. *NASSP Bulletin, 79*(571), 9–18.

Caine, R. N., & Caine, G. (1995). Reinventing schools through brain-based learning. *Educational Leadership, 52*(7), 43–47.

Caine, R. N., & Caine, G. (1990). Understanding a brain-based approach to learning and teaching. *Educational Leadership, 48*(2), 66–70.

Campbell, L., Campbell, B., & Dickinson, D. (1996). Teaching & learning through multiple intelligences. Needham Heights, MA: Allyn & Bacon.

Canady, R. L., & Reina, J. M. (1993). Parallel block scheduling: An alternative structure. *Principal, 72*(3), 26–29.

Canady, R. L., & Rettig, M. D. (1992). Restructuring middle level schedules to promote equal access. *Schools in the Middle, 1*(4), 20–26.

Canady, R. L., & Rettig, M. D. (1993). Unlocking the lockstep high school schedule. *Phi Delta Kappan, 75*(4), 310–314.

Canady, R. L., & Rettig, M. D. (1995). The power of innovative scheduling. *Educational Leadership, 53*(3), 4–10.

Canady, R. L., & Rettig, M. D. (1995). *Block scheduling: A catalyst for change in high schools.* Princeton, NJ: Eye on Education.

Canady, R. L., & Rettig, M. D. (1996). *Teaching in the block: Strategies for engaging active learners.* Princeton, NJ: Eye on Education.

Carnegie Council on Adolescent Development (1989). *Turning points: Preparing American youth for the 21st century.* Washington, D.C.

Carroll, J. M. (1989). *The Copernican plan: Restructuring the American high school.* Andover, MA: The Regional Laboratory for Educational Improvement of the Northeast and Islands.

Carroll, J. M. (1990). The Copernican plan: Restructuring the American high school. *Phi Delta Kappan, 72*(5), 359–365.

Carroll, J. M. (1993). The Copernican plan evaluated: The evolution of a revolution. *Phi Delta Kappan, 75*(2), 105–113.

Carroll, J. M. (1994). *The Copernican plan evaluated: The evolution of a revolution.* Topsfield, MA: Copernican Associates.

Carroll, J. M. (March, 1994) Organizing time to support learning. *School Administrator,* 26–33.

Cawelti, G. (1989). Designing high schools for the future. *Educational Leadership, 47*(1), 30–36.

Cawelti, G. (1994). *High school restructuring: A national study.* Arlington, VA: Educational Research Service.

Cawelti, G. (ed.). (1995). *Handbook of research on improving student achievement.* Arlington, VA: Educational Research Service.

Center for Applied Research and Educational Improvement (CAREI) (1995). *Report study for the four-period schedule for Anoka-Hennepin District No. 11*. Minneapolis, MN: College of Education and Human Development, University of Minnesota.

Conti-D'Antonio, M., Bertrando, R., & Eisenberger, J. (1998). *Supporting students with learning needs in the block*. Larchmont, NY: Eye on Education.

Conway, M. A., Cohen, G., & Stanhope, N. (1991). On the very long-term retention of knowledge acquired through formal education. Twelve years of cognitive psychology. *Journal of Experimental Psychology, General, 120,* 395–409.

Costa, E., & Taylor, E. (1998). *Breaking Ranks: Empirical Evidence for Block Scheduling*. Paper presented at the 82nd annual National Association of Secondary School Principals Convention, San Diego, CA.

Cunningham, Jr., R. & Nogle, S. A. (1996). Implementing semesterized schedule: Six key elements. *High School Magazine, 3*(3), 28–32.

Cushman, K. (1995). Using time well: Schedules in essential schools. *Horace 12*(2), 1–8.

Darling-Hammond, L. (1995). Restructuring schools for student success. *Journal of the American Academy of Arts and Sciences, 124*(4), 153–162.

Darling-Hammond, L., & McLaughlin, M. (1995). Policies that support professional development in an era of reform. *Phi Delta Kappan, 76*(8), 597–604.

Day, M. M., Ivanov, C. P., & Binkley, S. (1996). Tackling block scheduling. *Educational Leadership, 53*(5), 24–27.

Dempster, F. N. (1993). Exposing our students to less should help them learn more. *Phi Delta Kappan, 74*(6), 433–437.

Dow, J., & George, P. (1998). Block scheduling in Florida high schools: Where are we now? *NASSP Bulletin, 82*(601), 92–111.

Edwards, Jr., C. M. (1993). The four-period day: Restructuring to improve student achievement. *NASSP Bulletin, 77*(553), 77–88.

Edwards, Jr., C. M. (1995). Virginia's 4x4 high schools: High school, college, and more. *NASSP Bulletin, 78*(571), 24–25.

Edwards, Jr., C. M. (1995). The 4x4 plan. *Educational Leadership 53*(3), 16–19.

Eineden, D. V., & Bishop, H. L. (1997). Block scheduling the high school: The effects on achievement, behavior, and student-teacher relationships. *NASSP Bulletin, 81*(589), 45–54.

Ellis, A. K., & Fouts, J. T. (1993). *Research on educational innovations*. Larchmont, NY: Eye on Education.

Ellis, A. K., & Fouts, J. T. (1994). *Research on school restructuring*. Larchmont, NY: Eye on Education.

Ellis, A. K., & Fouts, J. T. (1997). *Research on school restructuring* (2d ed.). Larchmont, NY: Eye on Education.

Elmore, R. F., & Associates (1990). *Restructuring schools: The next generation of educational reform*. San Francisco: Jossey-Bass Publishers.

Evans, R. (1996). *The human side of school change: Reform, resistance and the real-life problems of innovation*. San Francisco: Jossey-Bass Publishers.

Faas, L. A., Lindsay, D., & Webb, L. D. (1997). *Personal plans for progress for secondary school students*. Reston, VA: National Association of Secondary School Principals.

Festavan, D. G. (1996). Flexible scheduling: Using time productively. *High School Magazine, 3*(3), 18–19.

Fitzgerald, R. (1996). Brain-compatible teaching in a block schedule. *School Administrator, 53*(8), 20–24.

Fitzpatrick, J. E., & Mowers, M. (1997). Success and the four block schedule: Stakeholders buy it! *NASSP Bulletin, 81*(588), 51–56.

Frederick, W. C., & Walberg, H. J. (1980). Learning as a function of time. *Journal of Educational Research, 73*: 183–194.

Fullan, M. (1991). *The new meaning of educational change*. New York: Teachers College Press.

Fullan, M. (1993). *Change forces: Probing the depths of educational reform*. London: The Palmer Press.

Fullan, M., & Miles, M. B. (1992). Getting reform right: What works and what doesn't. *Phi Delta Kappan, 73*(9), 744–752.

Gainey, D. D. (1993). *Education for the new century*. Reston, VA: National Association of Secondary School Principals.

Gainey, D. D. (1994). The American high school and change: An unsettling process. *NASSP Bulletin, 78*(560), 26–34.

Gainey, D. D. & Webb, L. B. (1998). *The education leader's roll in change: How to proceed*. Reston, VA: National Association of Secondary School Principals.

Gardner, H. (1983). *Frames of mind: The theory of multiple intelligences*. New York: Basic Books.

Gardner, H. (1991). *The unschooled mind: How children think and how schools should teach*. New York: Basic Books.

Gardner, H. (1995). Limited visions, limited means: Two obstacles to meaningful education reform. *Journal of the American Academy of Arts and Sciences, 124*(4), 101–106.

Gathercoal, P. (1990). Brain research and mediated experience. *Clearing House, 63*(6), 271–273.

Gatewood, T. E. (1989). Caution! Applying brain research to education. *Clearing House, 63*(1), 37–39.

Gilkey, S. N., & Hunt, C. H. (1998). *Teaching mathematics in the block*. Larchmont, NY: Eye on Education.

Glasser, W. (1990). *The quality school*. New York: Harper & Row.

Glickman, C. D. (1992). *Renewing America's schools: A guide for school-based action*. San Francisco: Jossey-Bass Publishers.

Goodlad, J. I. (1984). *A place called school: Prospects for the future*. New York: McGraw-Hill.

Goodlad, J. I., & Oakes, J. (1988). We must offer equal access to knowledge. *Educational Leadership, 45*(5), 14.

Goodman, J. (1995). Change without difference: School restructuring in historical perspective. *Harvard Educational Review, 65*(1), 1–29.

Guskey, T. (1990). Integrating innovations. *Educational leadership, 47*(5), 17–24.

Guskey, T. R., & Sparks, D. (1991). What to consider when evaluating staff development. *Educational Leadership, 49*(3), 73–76.

Hackmann, D. G. (1995). Ten guidelines for implementing block scheduling. *Educational Leadership 53*(3), 24–27.

Hackmann, D. G., & Schmitt, D. M. (1997). Strategies for teaching in a block-of-time schedule. *NASSP Bulletin, 81*(588), 1–9.

Hackmann, D. G., & Waters, D. L. (1998). Breaking away from tradition: The Farmington High School restructuring experience. *NASSP Bulletin, 82*(596), 83–92.

Hamdy, M., & Urich, T. (1998). Perceptions of teachers in south Florida toward block scheduling. *NASSP Bulletin, 82*(596), 79–82.

Hampel, R. (1986). *The last little citadel: American high schools since 1940*. Boston: Houghton Mifflin.

Hawley, W. D., & Valli, L. (1996, Fall). The essentials of effective professional development: A new consensus. *ASCD Professional Development Newsletter*.

Hirsh, S. (1997). Breaking Ranks recommendations require standards-based staff development. *High School Magazine, 4*(4), 4–13.

Hirsh, S. (1997). *Building effective teams*. Reston, VA: National Association of Secondary School Principals.

Hirsh, S., & Ponder, G. (1991). New plots, new heroes in staff development. *Educational Leadership, 50*(3), 43–47.

Hlebowitsh, P. S., Wraga, W. G., & Tanner, D. (eds.) (1996). *Annual review of research for school leaders*. Nw York: Scholastic Inc.

Hottenstein, D., & Malatesta, C. (1993). Putting a school in gear with intensive scheduling. *High School Magazine, 1*(2), 23–29.

Howard, E. (1998). Trouble with block. *American School Board Journal, 185*(1), 35–36.

Huff, A. L. (1996). Flexible block scheduling: It works for us! *NASSP Bulletin, 80*(580), 19–22.

Hurley, J. C. (1997). The 4 x 4 block scheduling model: What do teachers have to say about it? *NASSP Bulletin, 81*(593), 53–63.

Hurley, J. C. (1997). The 4 x 4 block scheduling model: What do students have to say about it? *NASSP Bulletin, 81*(593), 53–63.

Jakicic, C. (1994). Taking small steps to promote collaboration. *Journal of Staff Development, 15*(2), 16–18.

Janas, M. (1998). Shhhhhh, the dragon is asleep and its name is resistance. *Journal of Staff Development, 19*(3), 13–16.

Janas, M., & Gurganus, S. (1995). Staff development opportunities for teacher leaders. *Journal of Staff Development, 16*(2), 8–12.

Jensen, E. (1998). *Teaching with the brain in mind*. Alexandria, VA: Association for Supervision and Curriculum Development.

Jordan, S. E. (1996). Multiple intelligences: Seven keys to opening closed minds. *NASSP Bulletin, 80*(583), 29–35.

Joyce, B. (ed.) (1990). *Changing school culture through staff development*. Alexandria, VA: Association of Supervision and Curriculum Development.

Joyce, B., & Showers, B. (1980). Improving inservice training: The messages of research. *Educational Leadership, 37*(5), 379–385.

Joyce, B. R., & Weil, M. (1986). *Models of teaching*. Englewood Cliffs, NJ: Prentice Hall.

Kagan, S. (1990). *Cooperative learning: Resources for teachers*. San Juan Capistrano, CA: Resources for Teachers, Inc.

Kagan, S. (1990). *Same-Difference: A cooperative learning communication building structure*. San Juan Capistrano, CA: Resources for Teachers, Inc.

Kagan, S. (1994). *Cooperative learning*. San Clemente, CA: Resources for Teachers, Inc.

Kaplan, L. S. (1997). Professional development for restructuring: Teacher leadership for classroom change. *High School Magazine, 4*(4), 14–21.

Kramer, S. I. (1997). What we know about block scheduling and its effects on math instruction, part I. *NASSP Bulletin, 81*(586), 18–42.

Kramer, S. I. (1997). What we know about block scheduling and its effects on math instruction, part II. *NASSP Bulletin, 81*(587), 68–82.

Kruse, C. A., & Kruse, G. D. (1996). The master schedule and learning: Improving the quality of education. *NASSP Bulletin, 80*(580), 1–8.

Kruse, G., & Zulkoski, M. (1997). The northwest experience: A lesser road traveled. *NASSP Bulletin, 81*(593),16–22.

Lieberman, A. (1995). Practices that support teacher development: Transforming conceptions of professional learning. *Phi Delta Kappan, 76*(8), 591–596.

Lieberman, A. & Grolnick, M. (1997). Networks, reform, and the professional development of teachers. In A. Hargreaves (Ed.), *Rethinking educational change with heart and mind*. Alexandria, VA: Association for Supervision and Curriculum Development.

Lieberman, A., & McLaughlin, M. W. (1992). Networks for educational change: Powerful and problematic. *Phi Delta Kappan, 73*(9), 673–677.

Lieberman, A., & Miller, L. (1990). Restructuring schools: What matters and what works. *Phi Delta Kappan, 71*(10), 759–764.

Massachusetts Commission on Time and Learning (1995). *Unlocking the power of time*. Malden, MA: Massachusetts Department of Education.

Massachusetts Department of Education (1995). *The Massachusetts Curriculum Frameworks: Common Chapters*. Malden, MA: Author.

Mistretta, G. M., & Polansky, H. B. (1997). Prisoners of time: Implementing a block schedule in the high school. *NASSP Bulletin, 81*(593), 23–31.

National Association of Secondary School Principals (1995). *Breaking ranks: Changing an American institution*. Reston, VA: Author.

National Commission on Excellence in Education (1983). *A nation at risk*. Washington, D.C.: U.S. Department of Education.

National Education Commission on Time and Learning (1994). *Prisoners of time: Report of the National Education Commission on Time and Learning*. Washington, D.C.: U.S. Government Printing Office.

National Education Commission on Time and Learning (1994). *Prisoners of time: What we know and what we need to know*. Washington, D.C.: U.S. Government Printing Office.

National Foundation for the Improvement of Education (1996). *Teachers take charge of the education: Transforming professional development for student success*. Washington, D.C.: Author.

Newmann, F. M., & Wehlage, G. G. (1993). Five standards of authentic instruction. *Educational Leadership, 50*(7), 8–12.

Northeast and Island Regional Educational Laboratory (1998). *Block scheduling: Innovations with time*. Providence, RI: Author.

Powell, A. G., Farrar, E., & Cohen, D. K. (1985). *The shopping mall high school: Winners and losers in the educational marketplace*. Boston: Houghton Mifflin.

Queen, J. A., & Gaskey, K. A. (1997). Steps for improving school climate in block scheduling. *Phi Delta Kappan, 79*(2), 158–161.

Queen, J. A., Algozzine, R. F., & Eaddy, M. A. (1997). The road we traveled: Scheduling in the 4 x 4 block. *NASSP Bulletin, 81*(588), 100–105.

Queen, J. A., & Isenhour, K. G. (1998). *The 4x4 block schedule*. Larchmont, NY: Eye on Education.

Raphael, D., & Wahlstrom, M. W. (1986). The semester secondary school and student achievement results from the second Ontario interantional science study. *Canadian Journal of Education, 11*(2), 180–183.

Raphael, D., Wahlstrom, M. W., & Kass, H. (1986). Debunking the semestering: Student mathematics achievement and attitudes in secondary schools. *Canadian Journal of Education, 11*(2), 36–52.

Rettig, M. D., & Canady, R. L. (1998). High failure rates in required mathematics courses: Can a modified block schedule be part of the cure? *NASSP Bulletin, 82*(596), 56 65.

Robbins, C. B., & Geiger, P. (1996). Prisoners of scheduling? Creative ways to schedule the school day. *High School Magazine, 3*(3), 20–23.

Saphier, J., & Gower, R. (1997). *The skillful teacher: Building your teaching skills.* Carlisle, MA: Research for Better Teaching, Inc.

Sarason, S. B. (1982). *The culture of the school and the problem of change.* Boston: Allyn and Bacon.

Sarason, S. B. (1990). *The predictable failure of educational reform: Can we change course before it's too late?* San Francisco: Jossey-Bass Publishers.

Sarter, M., Bernston, G. G., & Cacioppo, J. T. (1996). Brain imaging and cognitive neuroscience. *American Psychologist, 51*(1) 13–21.

Schein, E. (1978). *Career dynamics: Matching individual and organizational needs.* Reading, MA: Addison-Wesley.

Schlecty, P. C. (1991). *Schools for the twenty-first century.* San Francisco: Jossey-Bass Publishers.

Schweiker-Marra, K. E. (1995). The principal's role in changing school culture and implementing school reform. *ERS Spectrum, 13*(3), 3–11.

Senge, P. M. (1990). *The fifth discipline: The art and practice of the learning organization.* New York: Doubleday/Currency.

Shanker, A. (Ed.). (1990). *Changing school culture through staff development.* Alexandria, VA: Association for Supervision and Curriculum Development.

Shortt, T. L., & Thayer, Y. V. (1995). What can we expect to see in the next generation of block scheduling? *NASSP Bulletin, 79*(571), 53–62.

Shortt, T. L., & Thayer, Y. V. (1997). A vision for block scheduling: Where are we now? Where are we going? *NASSP Bulletin, 81*(593), 1–15.

Silberman, C. E. (1970). *Crisis in the classroom: The remaking of American education.* New York: Random House.

Sizer, T. (1984). *Horace's compromise: The dilemma of the American high school.* Boston: Houghton Mifflin.

Sizer, T. (1992). *Horace's school: Redesigning the American high school*. Boston: Houghton Mifflin.

Slavin, R. E. (1983). *Cooperative learning*. New York: Longman.

Slavin, R. E. (1987). Mastery learning reconsidered. *Review of Educational Research, 57*(2), 175–213.

Slavin, R. E. (1990). *Cooperative learning: Theory, research, and practice*. Englewood Cliffs, NJ: Prentice-Hall.

Sousa, D. A. (1995). *How the brain learns*. Reston, VA: National Association of Secondary School Principals.

Sparks, D., & Hirsh, S. (1997). *A new vision for staff development*. Alexandria, VA: Association for Supervision and Curriculum Development.

Sparks, D., & Loucks-Horsley, S. (1989). Five models of staff development for teachers. *Journal of Staff Development, 10*(4): 40–57.

Speck, M. (1996). Best practice in professional development for sustained educational change. *ERS Spectrum, 14*(2), 33–41.

Staunton, J. (1997). A study of teacher beliefs on the efficacy of block scheduling. *NASSP Bulletin, 81*(593), 73–80.

Staunton, J., & Adams, T. (1997). What do teachers in California have to say about block scheduling? *NASSP Bulletin, 81*(593), 81–85.

Sylwester, R. (1990). An educator's guide to books on the brain. *Educational Leadership, 48*(2), 79–80.

Sylwester, R. (1990). Expanding the range, dividing the task: Educating the human brain in an electronic society. *Educational Leadership, 48*(2), 71–78.

Sylwester, R., & Cho, J. (1993), What brain research says about paying attention. *Educational Leadership, 50*(4), 71–75.

Tafel, L., & Bertani, A. (1992). Reconceptualizing staff development for systemic change. *Journal of Staff Development, 13*(4), 42–45.

Tewel, K. J. (1995). *New schools for a new century: A leader's guide to high school reform*. Delray Beach, FL: St. Lucie Press.

Toffler, A. (1990). *Powershift: Knowledge, wealth, and violence at the edge of the 21st century*. New York: Bantam Books.

U.S. Department of Labor (1991). *What work requires of schools: A SCANS report for America 2000*. Washington, D.C.: Author.

Wasley, P. A. (1997). Alternative schedules: What, how, and to what end? *NASSP Bulletin, 81*(588), 44–50.

Watts, G. D., & Castle, S. (1992, April). *The time dilemma in school restructuring*. Presented at the Annual Meeting of the American Educational Research Association, San Francisco, CA.

Willis, S. (1993). Are longer classes better? *ASCD Update, 35*(3), 1–3.

Winn, D. D., Menlove, R., & Zsiray, Jr., S. W. (1997). An invitation to innovation: Re-thinking the high school day. *NASSP Bulletin, 81*(588), 11–18.

Wolfe, P., & Brandt, R. (1998). What do we know from brain research? *Educational Leadership, 56*(3), 8–13.

Wood, J. W., & Rosbe, M. (1985). Adapting the classroom lecture for the mainstreamed student in the secondary school. *Clearing House, 58*(9), 354–358.

Wronkovich, M., Hess, C. A., & Robinson, J. E. (1997). An objective look at math outcomes based on new research into block scheduling. *NASSP Bulletin, 81*(593), 32–41.

Wuthrick, M. A. (1990). Blue jays win! Crows go down in defeat! *Phi Delta Kappan, 71*(7), 553–556.